PRAISE FOR *BELIEVER, BULLDOG, COACH*

Steve Smithwick combines his determination, faith, values, and personal experience to develop and articulate a proven strategy to win at life and business. This eye-opening, commonsense, and engaging read weaves the counsel from the heart of a coach and Christ follower to deliver insight you can apply each and every day.

—Ricky Smith
Lead pastor, Calvary Baptist Church

Whether you're launching your first venture, contemplating entrepreneurship, or leading as a seasoned CEO, *Believer, Bulldog, Coach* is an invaluable guide. Drawing on insights from acclaimed authors and his own experiences, Steve Smithwick weaves a heartfelt and inspiring narrative about building something meaningful while staying true to your principles.

—David McFarland
CEO and founder, Coterie Insurance

I've known Steve for many years. I've competed against him, I've tried to acquire him, and I've worked with him. He's a throwback to the old way of doing business, where his word or handshake is his bond. I know his story well, and you will find this book to be a fascinating read about a guy who beat the odds because he didn't believe in giving up.

—Buck Buchanan

Forty-year veteran of the EIFS industry; consultant; author

With *Believer, Bulldog, Coach,* Steve Smithwick offers an essential and heartfelt guide to perseverance in all aspects of faith, business, and family life. Having been in business with Steve for decades, I always hear him say the same thing to me EVERY time I see him: How is your family? How is your business? And thank you for the business. You may see yourself in these pages.

—Mike Chaney

President, James River Exteriors

In *Believer, Bulldog, Coach,* Steve Smithwick has managed to capture and, more importantly, share all the small things that add up to make a tremendous difference in our lives and careers, things we often miss because we are too busy trying to get it right. This is a must-read for anyone starting out or struggling to find a path forward by believing in themselves and their convictions. You will find yourself reading it more than once.

—Ted DeVit

President and founder, DeVit Consulting Inc.

The knowledge I have gained from Steve Smithwick has helped me build a hunger for His Likeness needed for success. In *Believer, Bulldog, Coach*, Steve shows people in all seasons of life how to balance resilience with vulnerability. Steve says it all here: "Watching people use their gifts and talents without being forced into a predefined mold is fascinating and rewarding."

—Ryan M. Carrick, PhD, MHS, OTR/L
Occupational therapist; assistant professor; legal therapy consultant

Steve Smithwick's book, *Believer, Bulldog, Coach,* provides a very realistic description of what a self-starter should expect on her/his path to personal and professional success. "Never, never, *never* give up" is the core attitude of what creates a successful person. It is a must-read for all future entrepreneurs.

—Flavio Ronzani

In *Believer, Bulldog, Coach*, Steve Smithwick offers an essential and heartfelt guide to hard work and life. I am thankful for Steve Smithwick and for the influence he has had on my life.

—Matthew T. Dalrymple
Head of school, Southwest Georgia Academy

As a consultant and manufacturing business owner, Steve's story and his experiences shared in *Believer, Bulldog, Coach* are powerful reminders to seasoned veterans while offering great wisdom on perspective and mindset for those just starting their careers or life journeys. It's an encouraging read on life's struggles, perseverance, faith, relationships, trials, and success.

—Derek Woodham
Associate director, Georgia Manufacturing Extension Partnership at Georgia Tech

Steve Smithwick's transparent story should be required reading for anyone who aspires to make a difference with their life. Steve's life illustrates the impact of having a clear vision built around faith, determination, and integrity—all this, combined with deep empathy for others, is powerful.

—Gary Bottoms, CLU, ChFC
Founder, Summit Legacy

Believer, Bulldog, Coach offers great words of wisdom and encouragement from Steve Smithwick, a man who not only states that he "values characteristics like loyalty, integrity, and transparency" but lives a life proving these characteristics define himself and his relationship with others. In his story, Smithwick gives tips and techniques for achievement, not only in success and business but in personal and family life as well. He has been a role model and mentor for many, and with his transparency and honesty in the telling of his story, he continues to provide encouragement and motivation to his readers.

—Nicholas Smith, DPM

As an account manager, this book will become an outstanding and trusted reference for managing complex projects as you navigate the challenges of team coordination and resource allocation. Steve Smithwick brings management principles to life in a realistic and simplified way that exceeds any previous educational attempts.

Truly I believe that Mr. Smithwick has many life lessons for all of us. When I think of Mr. Smithwick, I think of Dory's phrase from *Finding Nemo*: "Just keep swimming." Never give up on your dream.

—Dianna Renz

Senior account manager, Dow Construction Chemicals

Believer, Bulldog, Coach is uniquely realistic and a commonsensical approach to understanding not only what it takes to get where you want to go but also what it will take to get there. Steve's personal journey and decades of hard-fought experience are brought to life with authentic prose that will resonate with everyone who is at a pivotal moment in their lives. Moreover, the EIFS industry and I have seen firsthand the benefits of Steve's perseverance, resilience, and unshakable faith in his leadership at EIMA.

—Stephen Sears

CEO and executive director, EIFS Industry Membership Association

Living the Christian life requires genuine effort on the part of the individual. Steve Smithwick has detailed for the reader how perseverance, faith, and hope all work together to achieve a life well lived.

—Bob Gilson
Industrial Metal Fabricators, Inc.

I know Steve as a church member, brother, and friend. He overcame an unlikely start, was sabotaged early on, and survived unimaginable stress and odds to become a successful entrepreneur. Larry Burkett published ten biblical principles to follow in *Business by the Book*. Steve did all ten and is an example of what can happen when one does it God's way. You, too, can follow his example to experience the fulfilled life.

—Don Wilhite
DMin, pastor emeritus, Calvary Baptist Church, Columbus, Georgia

BELIEVER, BULLDOG, COACH

STEVE SMITHWICK

BELIEVER, BULLDOG, COACH

AN ENTREPRENEUR'S JOURNEY OF PURPOSE, PERSEVERANCE, AND LOVING PEOPLE

Advantage | Books

Published by Advantage Books, Charleston, South Carolina.
An imprint of Advantage Media.

Printed in the United States of America.

10 9 8 7 6 5 4 3 2

ISBN: 979-8-89188-173-0 (Hardcover)
ISBN: 979-8-89188-174-7 (eBook)

Library of Congress Control Number: 2025904677

Cover design by Megan Elger.
Layout design by Ruthie Wood.

04-10-2025 12:9

To my wife, Donnie Smithwick. This book would not have been possible if not for her constant help with grammar and relentless proofreading.

She is a constant in my life, with her dedication to our family and support for starting and growing Master Wall. Most of all, for the grace she has shown in our marriage and relationship. I'm constantly thanking God for her and her contribution to our fifty-one years of marriage.

CONTENTS

INTRODUCTION

Writing this book wasn't something I ever thought I'd do. I'm a builder by nature and someone who's spent his life rolling up his sleeves, getting things done, and letting his work speak for itself. But over the years, and especially as I've seen others face the same struggles I once did, I've come to realize that there's value in sharing where I've been, what I've learned, and how I managed to keep going when times got tough.

My hope is that this book reaches you at just the right moment—whether you're at a crossroads in your life, feeling the weight of a big decision, or needing a reminder that, no matter how dark things look, you can always move forward if you walk in faith and stick to your principles. This is my story, yes, but it's also a story that I hope will resonate with anyone who's ever been told they couldn't do it, anyone who's had to fight for every inch, and anyone who believes in the power of perseverance.

My journey isn't the typical success story. I didn't grow up in a family of entrepreneurs, inherit a fortune, or have a business degree or even a college education. Instead, what I had was a hardworking father who worked every day of his life in a factory and a grandfather who owned a gas station and taught me the value of hard work. There was no grand plan for my life, no path laid out for me. I just knew I wanted to build something that mattered, something that reflected my values and would give others a chance to feel proud of the work they do.

This path has been anything but easy or straightforward. In *Resilient*, John Eldredge writes, "The epicenter of our being is the deep longing to aspire for things that bring us life, to plan for those things, to take hold of them, to enjoy them, and start the cycle over as we aspire toward new things!"[1] This has been my story. I've seen my fair share of setbacks, long nights, challenges, and self-doubt. But in these pages, you'll also see the deep satisfaction, the hard-won victories, and the power of simple principles like integrity, honesty, and faith that have guided me every step of the way.

In 1987, I founded a company called Master Wall, which manufactures quality stucco, coatings, and exterior insulation and finish systems for residential and commercial projects. This company's goal is to provide our industry with the best quality products, backed by informed employees committed to service at a competitive price.

Today, Master Wall has multiple plants across the United States, produces millions in revenue, and has built a reputation in the industry for excellence. And while I am proud of what the company has become, I am most proud of how we got here—not through shortcuts or compromises, but through hard work, resilience, and a commitment to doing things the right way.

While it's easy to look at where we're at today and assume success came easily, the truth is that our success story was decades in the making. Master Wall went through some dark periods. There were times when I didn't know how I'd make payroll, days when it seemed

1 John Eldredge, *Resilient: Restoring Your Weary Soul in These Turbulent Times* (Nashville: Thomas Nelson, 2022), 2.

like every phone call brought another problem, and moments when the pressure felt overwhelming.

As Jim Collins notes, "Few successful start-ups become great companies."[2] This is because being successful takes more work and intentionality than ever anticipated. But each of those challenges, each of those obstacles, taught me something valuable. They taught me the importance of resilience, of never losing sight of my values, and of holding on to faith even when the future looked bleak.

Not only do I not have the perfect story, but I'm also far from a perfect person. I just know the value of putting my head down, building a strong team, and working in the same direction for years on end. I know what it means to stay true to who I am, have patience, build an organization that reflects my values, and have the privilege of making a difference in the lives of those around me.

Master Wall has been and will always be more than a company. It's my community and ministry—a place where relationships matter and where we can build something bigger than any one person's efforts. I always want our company to stand for integrity, respect, and commitment to quality—a place where customers and employees alike feel that they are part of something worthwhile. I want Master Wall to be a place where our company culture is not words on our website or pictures on the wall—it is how our people feel on Sunday night.

We don't just make a product; we make connections. We make connections with our customers, our employees, and our community. We're not just in business to make a living; we're in the business of making a difference. We want to create something that will outlast us all.

---

2 Jim Collins, *Good to Great: Why Some Companies Make the Leap ... and Others Don't* (New York: Harper Business, 2001), 120.

My hope is that these pages offer something of value to you, whether you're an aspiring entrepreneur, a leader, or simply someone looking for a bit of encouragement. So, let's get started, and may this story be a reminder that with the right principles, the right heart, and the willingness to persevere, you can build a life and a legacy that truly matter.

CHAPTER 1

Reach Your Tipping Point

DON'T FIX THE BLAME; FIX THE PROBLEM.

—DANIEL BURRUS

Can I build a strong business and still hold true to my values? This was the question I asked myself nearly forty years ago when I founded Master Wall—a company that has since grown into a $40 million business with plants in Lithonia, Georgia; Brookshire, Texas; and Payson, Utah.

As someone who never earned a bachelor's or master's degree, let alone a PhD, I never felt like the sharpest knife in the drawer. Quite the contrary. I grew up in humble beginnings in Marietta, Georgia, as the second of four children with three sisters. My father worked for General Motors as a paint superintendent. He was a tough disciplinarian who provided my first exposure to manufacturing and instilled a strong work ethic in me. My grandfather owned a Sinclair full-service gas station, and my time there pumping gas and washing windshields taught me the value of service and entrepreneurship.

After high school, I married at nineteen and started working for Aromatics International, a flavor and fragrance company. We made products that you could smell or taste, such as flavors for ice cream and scents for detergents. We used to say we made the smell or the taste, not the actual product. The owner, Lonnie Pope, turned out to be one of the people who influenced my work life the most.

Lonnie's approach was often chaotic and unstructured. Despite being a millionaire, he struggled with simple tasks like ensuring payroll was funded on time. However, leveraging his strengths, Lonnie excelled in building successful businesses through building strong relationships. This taught me a valuable lesson. It helped me see that trying to mold people into a specific model often limits their potential. Instead, recognizing their unique talents and placing them in roles that suit them allows them to thrive.

After a few years, R. J. Reynolds Tobacco Company purchased Aromatics International and expanded it significantly, making me the production manager in the process. But it wasn't long before R. J. Reynolds sold the business to a New Jersey–based company named Albert Verley. Choosing not to make the move north, I rejoined Lonnie, who had started a new flavor and fragrance business, Aromatic Fragrances and Flavors International, Inc. (AFF), in the same building.

This meant I ran straight back into chaos mode. Working for Lonnie was a wild experience. We'd create unique products like synthetic nuclear waste for E. I. du Pont and vanilla extracts from spent Coca-Cola vanilla beans. The pace was so frantic that the stress from this job led to me developing an ulcer, prompting me to look for other opportunities.

I sent a single résumé to a PO box in Columbus, Georgia, which turned out to be a company called Dryvit Systems. They hired me, and despite not fully understanding their business, I took the leap of faith and moved my family to Columbus. Lonnie Pope's parting words to me were memorable. "I hope someday you will have a business of your own," he said.

Little did he know how prophetic those words would be, for soon my world would turn upside down.

"YOU'RE FIRED"

Life at Dryvit started wonderfully, and for the first seven years, I was a plant manager. Frank Morsilli founded Dryvit, and he was the pioneer of the exterior insulation and finish system (EIFS) market. Dryvit was the first in the industry, with exceptional pricing and abundant resources.

Frank had probably the best marketing mind of anyone I've ever known. When he founded Dryvit in 1969, he started a whole new industry in the US. That said, Frank was an Italian with a fiery temper who managed by intimidation. He was so fiery that whenever he was in one of his moods, everyone knew to steer clear of him and warn unsuspecting employees that "Frank's chewing the rug"—code for *shut up and disappear*!

Frank, however, proved to be the least of my worries. In the summer of 1987, I was sent to South Korea to set up a manufacturing facility. Admittedly, I felt a little uneasy about taking this trip. My relationship with my regional manager was strained, and I worried about leaving our home facility for extended periods, fearing he would find a reason to fire me.

Upon my return, my fears were justified. I was called into a surprise meeting and told my contract was terminated. Despite the prior red flags, I was still stunned. It all happened so fast. One minute,

I was a plant manager for an EIFS manufacturer, traveling around the globe, and the next, I was told to turn in the company car keys and get my stuff out of my office desk before I left the building.

Seeing my shock, the VP tried to smooth things over and said, "I'll tell you what, I'll let you keep the car for thirty days, and then we'll get it back from you." A cold sweat ran down my face as I walked to the parking lot. I was married and had four children—the youngest of whom had not even turned one. *What will I do next? How will I support my family? Is my career over?* Despite my challenges with the regional manager, I'd always believed I had a secure future with Dryvit, but now everything was up in the air. Only an earned bonus that I fought for, consulting jobs, and my retirement savings kept my family afloat for the next few months.

It would take years to see how this painful experience was just the career change I needed.

OPPORTUNITY CALLS

In *The Fred Factor*, Mark Sanborn writes, "Don't wait for the perfect opportunity. Just take an opportunity and make it as perfect as you can."[3]

My opportunity, as it turned out, was just around the corner. After being fired, I took some consulting roles and had probably a dozen people reach out and encourage me to start my own company. "Steve, you know how to make a product," they said. "Why don't you start a business and make it yourself?" I trusted these individuals and had great relationships with many of them, so I took what they said seriously.

---

3 Mark Sanborn, *The Fred Factor: How Passion in Your Work and Life Can Turn the Ordinary into the Extraordinary* (New York: Currency Doubleday, 2004).

From my previous work in the EIFS industry, I believed in the products and the processes. I knew I could improve and continue to work in the field I loved. Because Dryvit was a more established company, I knew they might want to avoid taking on some of the risks a new start-up might be willing to take. This would give us a competitive advantage.

So, in December 1987, I saw my opportunity and took it. After navigating unemployment for several months, my two friends—Billy Joe Donaldson and Steve Davis—and I launched a company called Master Wall. This company now manufactures quality stucco, coatings, and EIFSs for residential and commercial projects. Our goal was simple: to provide our industry with the best quality products, backed by informed employees committed to service at a competitive price.

The pieces all fell into place quicker than I could have imagined. While at Dryvit, I had built great relationships with many of our customers, particularly some of the subcontractors. One of them, Billy Joe, had a large facility in Lithonia, Georgia, and he asked me to come there and make some material for him. I had a thirty-gallon mixing pot and a motor with only two speeds. Because of splash and very little motor speed control, I could only make a little over three five-gallon pails at a time.

First mixer with original branding look on bucket.

Little did I know that this was the building where my business would start and continue operating—to still be going almost forty years later. As a subcontractor, Billy Joe handled material and was a plasterer. He was also a strong, constructive critic—something every new business needs. I'd make material, and he'd say, "No, it needs to be smoother, more buttery; it's too rough." He was critical in the founding of Master Wall, and because he was already a large established contractor, it sure helped when he started using our material for his business.

Because Billy Joe's business used the building during the day, I would drive two hours and arrive around four in the afternoon, work through the night, and quit when his crew started arriving the following morning. For the first six to eight months, I worked alone at night. Eventually, my father began showing up occasionally to help me. It was quite the juggling act!

While Billy Joe helped with the warehouse space in Lithonia, my other partner, Steve, provided a small amount of warehouse space, free office space, and assistance from one of his secretaries. This proved critical for our opening months of operation.

Steve, Billy Joe, and I each had one-third ownership at the time. Our situation was about as bare-bones as one could get. We had no credit and no cash flow. Still, neither Steve nor Billy Joe charged me anything for rent for those first couple of years. I don't know how I would have made it without them. But make it we did.

While some may say this was blind luck, I believe two factors helped us exponentially. First, we had a relational mindset with our customers. We used to tell them that our company was big enough to meet their needs but small enough to know their name. The second factor was the hand of God. I don't know how else to describe it but to say that I sensed His activity all over our business.

DIVINE AFFIRMATION

I'll never forget the day we incorporated our business and became a C corp. I found an attorney with a great reputation, and to this day, I'm not even sure why he took it upon himself to incorporate us. His name was Cecil Cheves, and one day, Steve, Billy Joe, and I walked into Cecil's conference room and signed the papers (Cecil was our corporate attorney for those first ten years, and then he retired).

After we signed, Cecil did something that took us all by surprise. Once we had laid down our pens, Cecil said, "Why don't we pray and ask for God's blessing on your company?" He probably had no idea that a small gesture could mean so much, but his actions set the tone for our business. We wouldn't be just a business that operated for a profit. We would be one that had the right values and glorified God—like a ministry.

Four decades later, I get emotional as I write this and think about the many ways I've seen God's blessing on our company. That moment was pivotal and gave me confirmation that I was on the path God had intended for me. It was a divine affirmation of my journey. Cecil's unexpected act of faith resonated deeply, solidifying my belief that I was following God's will.

While I recognize it's not popular for business leaders to be so open about their faith, I want you, the reader, to understand that perseverance and faith are crucial during the lowest times. Part of perseverance is learning to keep moving forward when times are hard and never making big decisions when you're in a low time. Also, when facing discouragement and disheartenment, remember that God often sends timely help. In the early days, when I only had a few employees, every payday was a test of faith. By midweek, I often didn't know where the money would come from, but I trusted God. Miraculously, new customers or opportunities would arise just in time to meet payroll.

I've had other moments when things were tight, but God gave our business favor by sending a large distributor who provided some great business and much-needed cash flow. I do not doubt that such moments were divine interventions.

Things like this happened repeatedly, reinforcing my belief in God's faithfulness and provision. In fact, I believe so strongly in God's provision that I even included it as part of Master Wall's five-point mission statement. However, before I share this statement, let me tell you a story.

MEMBERS ONLY

During the early days of Master Wall, I decided to drive two days to an industry meeting in Phoenix, hoping to join the EIFS Industry Members Association (EIMA). I had rented a car for the trip, anticipating the long distance, and the 1,800-mile journey was stressful.

While in Phoenix, I stayed at the DoubleTree hotel where the meeting was held. Because it was during MLB spring training, I remember having breakfast and seeing the Oakland Athletics baseball team, including stars like Mark McGwire and José Canseco. Thinking back, this was the only positive of the day. I was in for a rude awakening; upon arrival at the conference, I discovered that the meeting was for members only and was turned away.

While this was not as devasting as being fired, I was still a bit crushed. Pulling myself together, I got back in my car and started driving back on I-40, thoughts swirling around in my head. As I drove, I had a lot of time to think—time to think about how I would treat people if I had a team, time to think about the company I wanted to create, and time to think about the person I wanted to become.

Pulling over to the side of the road, I pulled out a legal pad and started scribbling down ideas, crossing some out and adding others. I pulled over and wrote things frequently on the way back. Finally, I had a mission statement that I felt would serve my company and our customers well. I had five points that would shape the next forty years of my business career. Here they are, along with a few words of explanation.

MASTER WALL'S MISSION STATEMENT

Statement #1 | To manufacture the highest quality EIFS and related products (coatings, adhesives, etc.) available in the market. Producing quality products can bring tremendous satisfaction. The company can achieve its highest goals when each employee meets or exceeds expectations and does quality work. When that work and your products satisfy or even exceed the customer's needs, you will obtain more repeat business.

Statement #2 | To be the service leader of our industry in the region and areas where we market our products. Why does service matter? Your organization should always strive to be the most successful, innovative, and recognizable among other professionals and companies in your industry. Excellent customer service will establish a prominent and influential position in your field of business. The customer never forgets when you go the extra mile to meet their needs.

Statement #3 | To be respected in our industry because of honesty and integrity within our ranks. Workplace integrity will bring many positive results. It breeds honesty, loyalty, respect, and responsibility. Honesty and integrity are vital for accountability, ethical leadership, and principled decision-making.

Statement #4 | To encourage our employees to set the highest standards possible for their careers and their personal lives by supporting them through education, training, and sharing any God-given wisdom we may obtain. To compensate all employees in such a way that they can support themselves and their families in a comfortable manner. Encouragement to set the highest career standards on any level can lead to the overall betterment of your employees and your company. Sharing God-given wisdom means we will strive to see life from God's perspective and act accordingly.

Of course, we would not be the company we are without the efforts of our employees. One way we show appreciation for hard work is through compensation. Compensation includes bonuses, which are an integral part of our showing appreciation for exceptional work. We believe and emphasize that what is celebrated is repeated. If your employees feel valued and know you want them to be financially comfortable, morale will be boosted, which in turn fosters a positive work and home environment for each of them. As an example, I have noticed over the years the quality of vehicles that employees drive has improved greatly.

Statement #5 | To seek God's guidance in all decisions and to give Him glory for any results. This is the most important point. Our God is a God of order, and He wants us to live in peace, not turmoil, so we must cover every decision by asking for God's guidance and direction. In our actions, in our thought life, in everything we do, we are told to glorify the Lord. This should always motivate us to glorify Him rather than ourselves.

This statement came from my former pastor, Nelson Price, who married my wife and me. In every sermon, he started with a reference to Jesus Christ and ended with "To God be the glory." His consistent message left a lasting impact on me and my company.

It's tough to overstate how pivotal that car ride back from Phoenix was. It changed my entire perspective. As I write this book, nearly four decades later, I'm not just attending EIMA; I have served my second term as president. It's a testament to how far we've come, and while I'm proud of that achievement, it's more about demonstrating what's possible with determination and faith. This journey is a reminder that any success our company experiences is because of God.

Speaking at EIMA.

IT'S NOT ABOUT YOU

Certain moments change us forever. In *The Tipping Point*, Malcolm Gladwell explores how minor decisions and small actions can lead to significant, life-altering changes in our personal lives and businesses. He writes, "The Tipping Point is the moment of critical mass, the threshold, the boiling point."[4] These insignificant choices or events can accumulate and, once they reach this crucial threshold, unleash a powerful ripple effect that dramatically alters the course of events.

Gladwell compares this phenomenon to the way infectious diseases spread. They might start slowly with a single interaction, but once they hit the tipping point, they can expand rapidly and unpredictably, sweeping through populations in a transformative wave. He emphasizes that it's not always massive overhauls or grand strategies that drive significant change. Sometimes it's the simple things.

This is tough for us to comprehend. As Gladwell writes, "We have trouble estimating dramatic, exponential change. We cannot conceive that a piece of paper folded over fifty times could reach the sun. There are abrupt limits to the number of cognitive categories we can make and the number of people we can truly love and the number of acquaintances we can truly know."[5]

Looking back, there was no way I could have known how significant my tipping point would turn out to be. As I made that long drive back from Phoenix, I couldn't have envisioned how one small decision I made would have ripple effects for years to come.

I write this because maybe you're at your own tipping point. If you feel like you're in the position I was in forty years ago and you're nervous about what next step you need to take, it's critical to pause

---

4 Malcolm Gladwell, *The Tipping Point: How Little Things Can Make a Big Difference* (New York: Little, Brown and Company, 2000), 12.

5 Ibid., 257.

and identify your values. If faith isn't the center of your life, then what is? And if faith is the center, ask yourself the question we asked in the opening: *Can I build a strong business and still hold true to my values?*

Everyone's tipping point is different. Maybe you're having one right now, and that's why you're reading this book. Through sharing my story, I don't aim to make myself the perfect model to emulate. Instead, my goal is to offer hope and reassurance for your journey. Maybe you're experiencing tough times or longing to take a leap of faith to start your own business. Regardless, let this moment be a tipping point in your life. Take the pressure off yourself by remembering it's about creating something that's not all about *you*.

One of the reasons I can't take credit for my success is that I've benefited from so many others. I think of my mentor and pastor, Don Wilhite, who profoundly influenced me. I watched him establish a Christian school, retirement centers, and assisted-living facilities with limited resources. His perseverance and faith were exemplary, teaching me the importance of never giving up despite the challenges.

Through his example, I realized success is not just about personal effort but also about recognizing and relying on the support and guidance that comes from a higher power. Through faith, determination, and the willingness to accept help, even the most daunting obstacles can be overcome.

At Master Wall, we have embraced this philosophy for decades. We've focused on identifying each individual's talents, abilities, and spiritual gifts and placing them in the right roles. By allowing managers and supervisors to lead in their own way, we've seen better results. Watching people use their gifts and talents without being forced into a predefined mold is fascinating and rewarding.

We almost never fire anyone unless there's a significant ethical violation. We have many long-term employees because we find ways to use everyone's talents effectively. Our positions range from production and quality control to accounting, sales and marketing, and credit management. It's rare that we can't find a place for someone.

We're not just about one person; we're a team.

FOCUS ON YOUR PEOPLE

In today's world, job turnover is astonishingly high, with some statistics suggesting that people switch jobs every four years on average.[6] This means that even if you're not going through a career change now, chances are you will be at some point in the future.

The key is to identify what is important and remain laser-focused on your objective. One of my core values is "What you focus on prospers." Whether it's dealing with a cash crisis or any other problem, focusing on it is the key to resolving it. This philosophy, which I picked up from leaders like John Maxwell and Jon Gordon, has been a guiding principle in my life.

Unfortunately, many business leaders lack a proper focus. As John Eldredge writes, "Truth be told, most of us are faking our way through life. We pick only those battles we are sure to win, only those adventures we are sure to handle, only those beauties we are sure to rescue."[7] In doing so, we settle for a life of mediocrity. We give in to distractions and run in a hundred different directions.

But when you know what you value, everything else falls into place. I value characteristics like loyalty, integrity, and transparency. Transparency builds trust, and being transparent is essential in all

---

6 U.S. Bureau of Labor Statistics, National Longitudinal Survey of Youth 1979 (NLSY79) Summary Report, accessed November 14, 2024, https://www.bls.gov/news.release/pdf/nlsoy.pdf.

7 John Eldredge, *Wild at Heart: Discovering the Secret of a Man's Soul*, expanded edition (Nashville: Thomas Nelson, 2011), 50.

relationships, whether with coworkers, family, or friends. Without trust, it's impossible to lead effectively. In the words of Stephen Covey,

> There is one thing that is common to every individual, relationship, team, family, organization, nation, economy, and civilization throughout the world—one thing which, if removed, will destroy the most powerful government, the most successful business, the most thriving economy, the most influential leadership, the greatest friendship, the strongest character, the deepest love. On the other hand, if developed and leveraged, that one thing has the potential to create unparalleled success and prosperity in every dimension of life. Yet, it is the least understood, most neglected, and most underestimated possibility of our time. That one thing is trust.[8]

Trust is formed in many ways. Sometimes, it's by simply being thoughtful. At Master Wall, we strive to show we care about our employees. We recognize birthdays with cards and checks, hold Christmas parties for our facilities across the country, and support our employees during difficult times.

I've always believed that you need to love your people. This is what I focus on. Using empathy and care transforms how they interact with you. Whether in sports teams I've coached or in the workplace, caring about people makes a significant difference. In the words of John Maxwell, "Walk the halls slowly." Every day. Give team members an opportunity to see you. Give them a chance to ask you questions. Let them know you are present and with them.

---

8 Stephen M. R. Covey, *The Speed of Trust: The One Thing That Changes Everything* (New York: Free Press, 2006).

PERSEVERANCE IS THE KEY

If you've reached your tipping point, remember that you don't need a PhD to achieve success. All you need is a little grit and perseverance. Like you, I've experienced my share of self-doubts. After losing my job in 1987 and as I was preparing to start Master Wall, I had no steady income, and so many thoughts and emotions were running through my head.

Why did I get fired? Was I too difficult to work with? Will I have what it takes to regroup? How will I pay the bills and feed my family? Am I making the right decisions? These were all difficult questions to answer.

I was intimidated by the size, scope, and possible impact of the decision in front of me. If I chose the wrong path, it might lead to financial ruin. I lacked confidence and despaired at the time commitment it would require and how this might impact my wife and kids. But through it all, God was there, answering my prayers and helping me navigate my fears and emotions. In the words of Chris Akosa, "Play it down and pray it up."[9]

I recalled my father's career at General Motors, which spanned over thirty years. I thought that's how everyone should be—loyal and committed to one job for life. However, now that I look back, losing my job was a total shock, but it was the best thing that could have happened to me. It pushed me out of my comfort zone and led me to where I am today. I developed or discovered the gift of faith through my experiences.

Keep in mind that not everyone has the same unique talents that fit traditional roles. If you find yourself in a position where you doubt your abilities, it's crucial to have faith in your talents and seek

---

9 Chris Akosa, *Play It Down and Pray It Up: Strategic Warfare Prayers & Decrees for Deliverance, Healing & Breakthrough* (Independently Published, 2021).

environments that allow you to use them. My personal experience of losing a job and finding a better path reinforced this belief. Sometimes, the most challenging moments lead to the best opportunities.

In conversations, I've often said that as bad as certain days were, they were also the best days of my life. I didn't realize it at the time, but those challenges led to growth and better opportunities. A friend of mine, Gary Bottoms, wrote, "I've come to believe that experiencing hardship is beneficial to faith and development of empathy." Difficult times can lead to the best outcomes, and what doesn't kill you *will* make you stronger.

The key is to never, never, *never* give up.

CHAPTER 2

Never, Never, Never Give Up

THE WILL MUST BE STRONGER THAN THE SKILL.

—MUHAMMAD ALI

The phrase "giving up" was never part of my childhood vocabulary.

I was always trained to finish what I started. As someone who was an average student at best, the only reasons I went to school were to satisfy my parents, play sports, and date girls. That's the truth, even if people often laugh when I say it.

Starting in junior high, I participated in football, basketball, and track, with track being my favorite of the three. Friday night football games were amazing—even if I hated practice with a passion. The experience of having various coaches of different athletic backgrounds constantly pushing me to press through pain, do a little more, and never give up started shaping my mindset. For six years, I was immersed in this mentality, and this environment instilled in me a never-give-up attitude, which other life events later built upon.

I played football as a split end, defensive halfback, part-time offensive halfback, and defensive safety. I was exceptionally fast, which was a good thing, too, as I only weighed a whopping 150 pounds! I was an off-and-on starter in basketball until my last couple of years in high school. At each step, I was resilient and focused. But something snapped during my junior year of basketball, and I made a decision I'd live to regret.

The varsity coach, Jay Dye, wanted me to go back and play JV ball while I continued playing varsity. He thought I needed more experience and reps, but this wasn't on my radar, and after one practice, I quit. My mind was made up. A year later, I had a change of heart and wanted back on the team. Everyone told me returning wouldn't be possible, but I loved basketball and wanted to play my senior year. I went to Coach Dye and apologized. I told him I'd do whatever it took to return.

To my knowledge, I'm the only person he ever let come back after quitting, and he allowed me to play my senior year. As a small gesture of thanks for this act of mercy, I resolved *never* to make this same mistake again, and to this day, when I start something, I do whatever it takes to follow through. And because of Coach Dye's influence, I've given numerous team members second chances after they have quit or left my company.

Life, much like basketball, is a mental game. It's not just about physical ability or skill; it's about how you handle the ups and downs, the pressure, and the challenges that come your way. Muhammad Ali said it well: "The will must be stronger than the skill."

Following in Coach Dye's footsteps, I became a high school basketball coach at age forty-five and have since passed on many of the values instilled in me to younger generations.

As someone who was fast and tenacious on defense but never a great shooter, I always respected Coach Dye's choice to focus on my strengths and not my weaknesses. That decision taught me that sometimes mindset and determination make the difference, not just raw talent. Basketball teaches the importance of repetition, discipline, and focus.

I always preached to my players that the game of life is invariably won or lost in our heads. I'd often coach guys who had negative thinking habits, and my job was to help them rewrite that script. Many players over my years of coaching high school–age boys were extremely talented but had no classroom discipline or control of their emotions. Whether they came from tough backgrounds or had every privilege, the mental game was where they struggled most. Some would get so down on themselves that you'd see it immediately—they'd miss a shot and slam the floor, or nearly tip over a chair in frustration when I'd pull them out of a game. It was a clear sign that their mindset was their biggest obstacle.

But as a coach, I knew consistency, discipline, and the right mental habits could turn things around. We emphasized routines, such as taking three dribbles before every free throw, because repetition helps build mental strength. One of my players even had a ritual where he'd picture someone important to him before every shot. It wasn't just about technique; it was about getting his mind in the right place every single time. By the end of the season, most of them had learned to stay levelheaded under pressure.

In the end, whether in basketball or life, it's our mindset that determines our success.

THE DISCIPLINE OF SELF-TALK

One of the little life secrets I've learned is that the key to not giving up is to discipline how you think and talk to yourself.

By the time I reached my mid-twenties, I was married, and my wife and I were expecting our first child. Suddenly, the weight of being a father was more than I could handle, and I realized that to avoid making some of the mistakes I'd seen my own dad make, I needed to think and act differently. I had a lot of work to do. The thought of it all was incredibly stressful, so much so that I became depressed, started having panic attacks, and went through several months of being a complete wreck, somehow managing to keep my job and function.

Amid this storm, a friend of mine, out of the blue, took her own life. Her death shook me, and I knew I needed to find a way to deal with the stress and the emotional toll it took on me. Before that point, I'd never been much of a reader, but I immersed my mind in positive self-help inspiration. I became a sponge for information and devoured the motivational words of authors like Norman Vincent Peale and Robert Schuller.

I read quotes by Peale that said things like, "Be so strong that nothing can disturb your peace of mind. Talk health, happiness, and prosperity to every person you meet. Make all your friends feel there is something special in them. Look at the sunny side of everything. Think only the best, be as enthusiastic about the success of others as you are about your own."[10] I read thoughts by Robert Schuller like, "Never cut a tree down in the wintertime. Never make a negative decision in the low time. Never make your most important decisions when you are in your worst moods. Wait. Be patient. The storm will pass. The spring will come."[11]

---

10 Goodreads, "Quotable Quotes: Norman Vincent Peale," accessed February 18, 2025, https://www.goodreads.com/quotes/163748-be-so-strong-that-nothing-can-disturb-your-peace-of.

11 Sydney Trent, "10 Quotations from the Late Rev. Robert H. Schuller That Could Inspire Anyone," *Washington Post*, April 2, 2015, https://www.washingtonpost.com/news/inspired-life/wp/2015/04/02/10-quotations-from-the-late-rev-robert-h-schuller-that-could-inspire-anyone/.

My former pastor, Don Wilhite, whom I mentioned previously, always sent a birthday card to every person in the congregation on their birthday (several hundred people). He always wrote, "You are special," on my card. That was quite encouraging. I try to remember to always write in my twelve grandkids' (also one great-grandchild's) birthday cards, "You are special."

I also memorized a lot of scripture, prayed, and tried to flood myself with things that might pull me out of my dark place. Over time, my self-talk increased my confidence so much that I could convince myself of almost anything. I became hyper-focused and knew I could finish whatever I started. A few years ago, I found a book titled *What to Say When You Talk to Your Self* by Shad Helmstetter, a book I wish I had found when it was first written. It's a short, interesting read, and one of the statements Helmstetter makes is,

> After you examine the philosophies, the theories, and the practiced methods of influencing human behavior, you'll find, as I did, that it gets down to the simplicity of one small but powerful fact: You will become what you think about most; your success or failure in anything, large or small, will depend on your programming—what you accept from others, and what you say when you talk to yourself.[12]

12 Shad Helmstetter, *What to Say When You Talk to Your Self* (New York: Park Avenue Press, 2011), 7–8.

THE JOB MUST GO ON

Reading this statement reminded me of my dad. During some of his most stressful times as an employee at General Motors, he would walk around telling himself, "I can do it." He practiced the art of self-talk before it was even a popular concept, and this left a lasting impression on me. The pressure of doubt can be a horrible obstacle to overcome, especially when you're tired, lonely, and exhausted. I was exhausted—sometimes working until four in the morning, making the material, putting it in buckets, and stacking everything. In those early days, I worked all night, often alone, until my dad stepped in to give me a hand.

Come to think of it, Dad was the first person to instill in me this never-give-up mindset. Growing up, he was tough and demanding, always pushing me to improve. I wasn't always up for this challenge, and by my teenage years, I had started rebelling because his expectations felt impossible to meet. He didn't just want me to get passing marks in school; he wanted me to excel.

Because he was a "take charge" kind of guy, I never told him I was starting Master Wall. That's why I was shocked when he opened the door one night and said he was there to give me a hand. Apparently, my mom had filled him in and let him know the stress I was under. To his credit, he was a willing student and a big help. He didn't know the processes or production methods, so he had to listen and learn, which wasn't easy for him. But there was a genuine desire to help, even if it was on his own terms.

By then, my dad was in his late sixties, had already retired from General Motors, and had started a second career. His health wasn't great, and he had to take nitroglycerin tablets to manage chest pain. Despite his limitations, he was determined to be involved. He would come by for a few hours and help me start things. Even though he couldn't stay all night, his presence was a huge support.

One event in particular spoke of the kind of man he was and his never-give-up attitude. Several years into Master Wall, we'd switched to working some afternoon shifts, and Dad was working at the plant. Suddenly, he reached for his chest, and it was only later I discovered he'd had a heart attack. I asked him if he was OK and said I'd close down work to drive him to the hospital. But he wouldn't hear of it. To him, I had to keep working. The job wasn't finished. So, he popped a few nitroglycerin tablets in his mouth and somehow drove himself to Emory University Hospital.

That extreme example shows his level of persistence, and I'll always be grateful to my dad for instilling in me the desire to keep moving forward—even when everything seems to say you can't.

LEARNING THE VALUE OF POSITIVE SELF-TALK

When I started Master Wall, there were many reasons I could have given up before I even got started. In my fifth or sixth year of working long days, I'd come home late, worn out, and missing time with my family. One night, I hit a breaking point. I was completely exhausted and overwhelmed. But in that moment, it was my mindset that saved me. I had to tell myself that things would get better and that it wouldn't always be this hard. That self-talk kept me going when everything inside of me wanted to quit. It sparked new energy in me.

In *The Energy Bus*, Jon Gordon writes, "Positive energy is like muscle. The more you use it the stronger it gets. The stronger it gets the more powerful you become. Repetition is the key and the more you focus on positive energy the more it becomes your natural state."[13] Such has been my experience. This energy was especially important during the first few years of Master Wall's existence.

Perhaps worst of all was the pressure of the daily grind. For the first four years, I'd leave home when the kids were getting back from school, say a quick hello and goodbye, and then head out, arriving at work to dive right in and start working. There were drums of acrylic, and bags of sand, clay, and other materials that were used in formulations. The work was very physical; other than the electronic scales and forklift, it was all manual work.

Eventually, I financed a ribbon blender (an industrial mixer) by putting my house up as collateral. This was a massive help. Billy Joe had let me use his forklift and one of his workers, a retired AT&T technician named Jay Bonner.

Jay was like an angel who walked into my life just when I needed him. He was incredibly responsible and could do anything. He was consistent, knowledgeable in algebra, and could even handle my formulas. In the EIFS business, especially back then, everything was custom-made for specific colors and textures. I had to learn color matching, and Jay quickly picked it up, helping me tremendously. For the first time, I felt like I could step away for thirty minutes or an hour, and everything wouldn't fall apart without me around. At this point, I began hiring temporary employees from a temp agency.

When I finally got the ribbon blender, we could make thirty pails at a time. A pallet held twenty-seven five-gallon pails, so we'd yield twenty-seven to twenty-eight pails per batch. We used construction scaffolding with two-by-twelve boards to stand on to pour and add material to the blender. A butterfly valve at the bottom of the blender

---

13 Jon Gordon, *The Energy Bus: 10 Rules to Fuel Your Life, Work, and Team with Positive Energy* (Hoboken: Wiley, 2007).

below allowed us to fill and weigh out what we had made. My thirty-gallon pot had a variable-speed motor with two settings, and when I first added material, it would splash until there was enough to settle it down. It was a very messy operation. I'd make three pails at a time, scoop and weigh the material into each pail, then start on the next batch. After adding the ribbon blender, I could make three batches or almost ninety pails a night, which was a big increase.

Ribbon cutting for new blender at the Utah manufacturing facility with Plant Manager Jeff Muir.

If you've ever mixed a bag of concrete from the store, you have an idea of what it was like. I'd add the materials, and if everything was too liquid, I'd adjust the ratios. The acrylic made it flexible, the sand provided texture, and the clay filled it in. There were various chemicals, such as bactericides and fungicides, that were used. Ethylene glycol was also used to prevent freezing.

I could manage about thirty to forty pails a night with the two-speed mixer, which was just enough to cover a residential job. After a full night of production, I'd load everything into the station wagon I'd financed—which I later upgraded to a van after going through several rear axles—and left Lithonia around five or six in the morning to drive back to Columbus. From there, I unloaded these pails into a small warehouse space for our customers and sped home just in time to see my kids before they went to school.

Eventually, we transitioned to daytime production, and Billy Joe gave me 25 to 30 percent of his building for production and office space. This gave me more flexibility and meant I could leave late afternoon, receiving occasional help from Billy Joe's employees and a few temporary employees I would hire. I'd try to get back home before my kids went to bed, and if I was lucky, they'd help me unload the pails. Even just rolling them to the door was a big help!

Despite the positive growth, it was still a grind. Even when I started working during the day, I'd leave home around six in the morning, arrive at the plant around eight thirty, and then work until closing—which could run as late as eight at night. I kept up this pace for three to four years. It wasn't until the fifth year, when Jay had essentially become my production manager, that I started to feel more comfortable coming in later or occasionally skipping a day to focus on office work in the Columbus office.

This pace was draining, and I often felt guilty because I wasn't there for my kids, especially during those first few years when I wanted to be. Thankfully, my wife was incredibly strong through it all, always supportive. She handled everything for the kids—taking them to school, helping with homework, and more.

As my children got old enough to play baseball, cheer, and do other activities, I finally reached a point where I could adjust my schedule and be there for them. But those first four or five years, it was nearly impossible, and I had to be careful how I spoke to myself. I couldn't let my self-doubt or fear of failure consume my thoughts. I had to stay positive and focused on the mission.

NO OTHER OPTIONS

One of the things that kept me grounded was that I didn't give myself the option to quit. While some might look back on my schedule and think I was working myself into the ground, you have to understand that in the 1980s, this was just the cost of doing business. I certainly wasn't that unusual.

My dad, for example, worked eighteen-hour days at General Motors with no flexibility. All bosses cared about was if you could get the job done. I worked for numerous employers who were the same way. Work was your life. Do I have some regrets? Sure. Were there some kids' sporting events I missed that my wife had to cover? Absolutely. In fact, the first decade of Master Wall's existence was tight and hard.

As someone who did some side consulting to make ends meet, I'll never forget the time I worked with a group out of New England. These were people I'd worked with while I was still at Dryvit, but since then, they'd left Dryvit and asked me to consult with them. They were trying to start a business for a guy in Texas who was paying them to help him compete. In good faith, I gave them the equipment information and the formulas I had developed at Master Wall. They paid me a couple of times, and things were going well.

Then I sent them an invoice for over $10,000, and everything grew eerily quiet. After three or four months, one of them called me and said, "I'm sorry, Steve. The reason we went quiet on you is that someone took money from our business, and we can't pay you." At a time when I desperately needed that money, those words felt like a hearty blow.

Nothing seemed easy. I knew production and the process of making a good product for a wall system, but I had so much to learn about doing business and running a business. After creating the products we needed, I had to find quality customers—people who could run their businesses well enough to actually pay Master Wall.

When you're the new business on the block, knowing who to work with and who to avoid is tough. For example, I quickly realized there were many subcontractors who were willing to use our product if I was willing to extend them credit. We literally had to act like a bank loaning money. Giving credit is like a short-term loan. When you don't have much cash flow, it is very risky.

After many interactions, it also became obvious that there was a reason my competitors wouldn't give them credit and why these subcontractors came to a guy like me who would. Experiences like these taught me so many painful and expensive lessons.

Then, there was the constant fear of competition. Before I bought the ribbon blender, while I was still working out of a corner in Billy Joe's building, rumors started circulating that the competition had caught wind of what we were doing. A couple even showed up at Billy Joe's facility, curious to see what was going on. Anticipating this, Billy Joe had covered everything up with foam and other materials so they couldn't see what was happening. Since it was such a small operation, it wasn't too tough to hide. Still, this always made us a bit nervous. I feared they would find some reason to sue me and stop Master Wall from competing with them.

While times like these weren't easy, I can honestly say I never seriously considered quitting. I just didn't give myself that option. Instead, I continued to fill my mind with positive voices, challenge my thinking, and resolve to never, never, never give up. I leaned into my pillars of tenacity, faith, and integrity—both in life and in business.

This never-give-up mindset extended well beyond my workplace. While I've been married for over fifty years, my wife and I, like every couple, have had our share of challenges. Raising kids has been another adventure. There have been moments of shocking disappointment and incredible joy. We've faced some incredibly tough circumstances, things that might have ended other marriages. But we never gave up; we just kept plowing through. We both had this outlook, and in our minds, there was no other option.

THE WORK-LIFE BALANCE MYTH

There is a lot of talk today about the importance of work–life balance. I get it. It's good to have healthy rhythms and a sustainable pace of life. But I'd also offer a word of caution. Sometimes there are seasons that are a bit extreme, such as starting a new business or launching a new initiative. You crave balance and having the ability to do those things you once did when you worked your nine-to-five job, but you can't. The only option is to push through and get the job done.

When I was working at Dryvit, I had a solid routine: I'd run in the mornings, shower, and start my day feeling refreshed. But when I started my own business, that routine fell apart. Exercise took a backseat for years because the work needed every bit of my focus and energy. It wasn't until later—once the dust settled—that I could rebuild those healthy habits and make room for a balanced life again.

To be a successful entrepreneur, you have to be a bit crazy. Not too crazy, but a little doesn't hurt. You must be willing to do those things others won't. This is me to a fault. I'm the kind of person who will always go too far. I'll overwork, sacrifice rest, and let stress pile up if that's what it takes to keep things moving. While this can be a fault, this mindset served me well in the early days of Master Wall.

That's not to say I didn't have certain parameters. Even in those hardest times, I knew some things couldn't be compromised. I almost never worked Sundays, instead prioritizing being in church and spending Sunday afternoons with my family. Occasionally, on Saturdays, I could make time for the kids. I would prepare breakfast when I could be there and then head to the office in Columbus. After about six years, the business stabilized, and I finally started setting up healthier rhythms, like scheduling important family events and being present when it mattered. But those rhythms didn't come until I got through the grind of those early years.

Life comes in seasons, and sometimes, we just have to push through the chaos. But once we get through it, that's when it's time to establish better rhythms and take care of ourselves and others.

NEVER, NEVER, NEVER GIVE UP

Today, I have a plaque on my desk that reminds me I can do it. It's etched with this statement: "Never, never, never give up."

I first heard these wise words from my former pastor, Don Wilhite, and they're a variation of Winston Churchill's speech he shared on October 29, 1941, at Harrow, a London boarding school. "Never give in. Never give in," he said. "Never, never, never, never—in nothing, great or small, large or petty—never give in, except to convictions of honour and good sense. Never yield to force. Never yield to the apparently overwhelming might of the enemy."[14]

Don Wilhite was the epitome of persistence and determination. He simply never gave up, no matter how challenging the circumstances. Don and I became close friends over the years. He bought a small farm near where I live, and we served on various committees together at our church. I watched him lead with unwavering dedication, especially when he was trying to launch the Christian school, the assisted-living and memory care facility, and Calvary Community, a retirement center.

None of these projects were easy. The church couldn't fund them alone, so Don had to go out and raise money, finding investors who believed in his vision. Whenever he faced difficult challenges, I often heard him say those five words: "Never, never, never give up." He was relentless and often joked that he was known as the biggest nonprofit beggar in Columbus, Georgia. He wasn't ashamed of it either; he fully believed in hard work and often quipped, "What's a four-letter word for fun?" Before anyone could respond, he'd say, "W-O-R-K. Work!"

Even now, in his eighties, Don still works on his farm like a man half his age. He used to be a runner, just like I was, and we grew even closer during our Sunday afternoon runs. After Sunday morning service, we'd change out of our church clothes and run the five miles back to our homes, which were in the same area. Those runs allowed me to know Don and understand his character even better. He still walks five miles a day. I often see him taking his walk in our neighborhood.

---

14 National Churchill Museum, "Never Give In, Never, Never, Never, 1941," accessed November 14, 2024, https://www.nationalchurchillmuseum.org/never-give-in-never-never-never.html.

Don was fiercely loyal and was persistent in words *and* action. When he first worked to get the second location of the church off the ground, he would show up on Saturdays to set up chairs in the gym, which served as our worship center. Often, he'd do this menial task alone. Still, Don would be there every Saturday, ensuring everything got done. Don always seemed to have more energy than anyone else. He was a model of what it means to push through challenges, to keep going when others would quit, and to create something lasting through sheer determination and faith.

Today, whenever I look at my desk and see those words, "Never, never, never give up," I think to myself, *If those words are good enough for Don Wilhite and someone who helped turn the tide of World War II, they are certainly good enough for me!*

INSTINCTS ARE KEY TO NEVER GIVING UP

So, how do you develop this never-give-up mindset? Part of it can be taught, but a large part is instinctual.

If you don't have a lot of formal education, something else must guide you, and that's where instincts come in. Instincts are often rooted in experience. I've had PhDs and engineers with master's degrees work at Master Wall who lacked common sense. I've heard it said that people equate education with being right, but this doesn't always hold true. Sadly, if someone doesn't have the right instincts, the value they add is limited. Instincts are huge. I often think of my oldest son, Steven. He's the only one out of my three boys who didn't get a degree, but he is exceptionally smart and has great instincts because of his life experiences.

Instincts are tricky to pin down, but I believe they are a mix of nature and nurture. Some people seem to be naturally wired with good instincts, but for most of us, it's something we catch through experience. When I talk with people who rely heavily on data, the concept of instinct baffles them. They want all the numbers lined up before making any move, while I might say, "My gut tells me we should do this."

That often gets me puzzled looks, especially in church leadership or business meetings. I've found that sometimes you must take that leap, trust your instincts, and see where things land. I'm not saying I'm always right—sometimes I'm wrong—but I trust my gut more often than not.

While I am not a natural risk-taker, I am a man of faith. To me, faith and instincts are closely connected. As a Christian, I believe that the Holy Spirit guides people to make wise decisions, and I do my best to be sensitive to His voice or slow to a neutral pace, as recommended in the book *Sacred Pace*.[15]

Again, sometimes I get this wrong, not because the Holy Spirit is wrong but because I am not patient enough to listen well. The Holy Spirit is never wrong. But if I only waited to make a decision until I was 100 percent certain, I would miss out on so many opportunities. Waiting for a perfect sign before making a move isn't really faith. True faith is about stepping out and trusting that the decision is right, even if everything isn't crystal clear. I also know to be patient when needed.

Looking back at the early days of Master Wall, there were plenty of instinctual decisions that paid off. Hiring people like Jay Bonner didn't make much sense on paper because I couldn't justify the salary at the time. But I knew I needed help, and I took the risk. As a result, Jay's productivity allowed me to focus on other areas, which became a game changer. My instincts told me to take a chance and hire a guy

---

15 Terry Looper, *Sacred Pace: Four Steps to Hearing God and Aligning Yourself with His Will* (Nashville: Thomas Nelson, 2019).

named Glen Smith to help me with some night shift work. He was a young guy I didn't know well, but I trusted Jay's recommendation, and Glen has been a key part of the team ever since. Today, nearly forty years later, he is our R&D manager and a critical member of our team.

When I look at how instincts play out, I realize it's more about personality and experience. Some people need every detail mapped out, and they're crucial for any organization. But you also need people who can see the big picture and guide the vision. That's where instincts come in. Having good instincts doesn't mean you are a *reckless* risk-taker. It means you take *calculated* risks and aren't paralyzed by fear.

For instance, a few months ago, Master Wall had a chance to buy a business. Our CFO said we couldn't afford it, but I felt strongly that we should move forward. We did, and it turned out to be a great decision. My COO wasn't thrilled because he knew he'd have to figure out how to make it work, but it was worth it in the end.

While I have some disagreements with his theology, I've found T. D. Jakes's book *Instinct* very helpful. In it, he writes, "Hardship can humble you, but it cannot break you unless you let it. Your instinct for survival will see you through if you're attuned to its frequency. Instinct will find a temporary stopgap without ever taking its sights off your larger goals. There's no greater way to hone your instincts than to overcome adversity."[16]

If you're doing something hard, your mind will convince you of a hundred and one reasons to give up. This is when you must fall back on your instincts and trust your gut. Remember, there was a reason you started what you started. Don't shortchange yourself. Sometimes, pressing a little harder is all it takes to break through.

---

16 T. D. Jakes, *Instinct: The Power to Unleash Your Inborn Drive* (New York: FaithWords, 2014).

CHAPTER 3

Face Your Near-Death Experiences

FAILING DOESN'T MEAN YOU ARE A FAILURE ... IT JUST MEANS YOU HAVEN'T SUCCEEDED YET.

—ROBERT SCHULLER

Because every entrepreneurial journey involves a series of peaks and valleys, it's important to develop a never-quit attitude.

The path to success is rarely a straight line. Instead, it's a winding road filled with unexpected detours, obstacles, and setbacks. Life is hard, especially when you're creating a new business. It feels like one challenge after another hits you in a wave, each one testing your resolve and determination. In those moments, you must know how to handle these challenges without losing perspective. During the toughest times, your character is truly tested, and your ability to persevere becomes the defining factor between success and failure.

When you're in a valley, it's easy to despair. The weight of difficulties can feel overwhelming, making it hard to see a way forward. The temptation to give up is strong, but that's precisely when you need to reset, refocus, and keep moving forward. It's in the valleys that your resilience is forged. In the words of American poet Maya Angelou, your "mission in life is not merely to survive, but to thrive; and to do so with some passion, some compassion, some humor, and some style."

By enduring the hardships and continuing to press on, you build the strength and wisdom necessary to climb the next peak. Every valley is an opportunity to learn, to grow, and to prepare for the challenges that lie ahead. Do this long enough, and you'll hit the next peak, a moment of triumph that makes all the struggles worthwhile.

Reflecting on the many challenges I faced while building Master Wall, one key Bible verse kept me going. It's Philippians 4:13 (New King James Version [NKJV]), which says, "I can do all this through him who strengthens me." This verse became my lifeline, a constant reminder that I wasn't alone in my struggles. It reassured me that no matter how insurmountable the obstacles seemed, I could rely on God's strength to carry me through.

As you read this chapter, you'll understand why this verse is so significant. It was only by God's strength that my company survived. The challenges were beyond what I could handle on my own, but with God's help, I persevered and ultimately succeeded.

Just the thought of some of these experiences makes me sick to my stomach. They were that tough. The memories of those dark times still linger, reminding me of the emotional and physical toll they took on me and everyone involved. But despite the difficulty, I can say with confidence that I experienced God's strength in ways I never could have imagined. Each trial deepened my faith, teaching me to trust God more fully and depend on Him in every situation. Through these experiences, I became stronger, both as a person and as a leader.

Life as an entrepreneur can be a struggle. It's not for the faint of heart, and there are moments when the pressure and stress seem unbearable. But when you have a never, never, never-give-up mindset, you can journey through even the darkest valleys. This mindset is what separates those who succeed from those who falter. It's the ability to keep going, to push through the pain, and to refuse to quit, no matter how dire the circumstances. This determination, fueled by faith and perseverance, is what ultimately leads to victory.

There were three times when Master Wall was close to shutting its doors. I like to call these our "near-death experiences." Each one was a crisis that threatened the very existence of the company, forcing us to confront our deepest fears and find a way to survive. The first of these was triggered by what we might call "the grand pyrite mystery."

THE GRAND PYRITE MYSTERY

Master Wall uses sand in nearly all of its products except for a few paints. Within these sands, sometimes there were veins of iron ore called pyrite. When pyrite ends up in a finished product, it causes major problems down the line.

After a couple of years, the pyrite reacts to moisture and sunlight, eventually erupting from the wall in small, pencil-tip-sized bursts. As it does, streaks begin forming on the wall—starting as reddish-brown and eventually turning white. These streaks can range from a few inches to several feet long, depending on the pyrite concentration in the sand. The result is a surface covered with unsightly spots, almost like measles on an exterior wall.

We did everything we could to catch these impurities, using tools like rare-earth magnets. But since pyrite isn't magnetic, it slipped through. As the issues became more widespread, we started getting calls from customers, and when I saw the damage firsthand, I knew we had a serious problem.

To address this problem, we hired crews to manually remove the spots—a process we called "pick and clean." Workers would go out with small knives or cordless drills, picking out the spots one by one. After removing the spots, the walls had to be washed and sometimes repainted. In some cases, that worked, but most times, the walls still needed recoating.

At first, we didn't involve insurance because we didn't know how big this issue would get. The cost of repairs ranged from $5,000 to $20,000 per job, and we tackled them as we could over the next three to five years. It was especially challenging because we were a small, young company in the early '90s with limited resources.

Somehow, we managed to keep our heads above water. Thankfully, customers weren't suing us, but they were demanding we fix the problem. We did everything we could to address their concerns, sometimes repairing and repainting the same houses two or three times at no cost to the owner. Financially, it was a significant burden, and we didn't know where we'd find the money.

Eventually, after several years of trial and error, someone gave us a tip to use a sodium nitrate solution that stopped the pyrite from reacting. This was a game changer and transformed everything overnight.

But even as one crisis was averted, another arose. Competitors were always looking for a leg up on the competition, and to compete in the commercial market, we needed specific building code certifications. Competitors would spread rumors that we didn't have the necessary code reports, telling contractors they'd be at risk if they used our products. At the time, we were focused on getting our Southern Building Code certification. I hired a man named Ted DeVit, whom I'd worked with at a previous company, to handle the testing. We invested thousands of dollars in fire testing, weathering tests, and other assessments until we finally received our SBCCI certification. Finally, we succeeded.

But just when we thought we were in the clear, we faced new hurdles as we tried to expand outside the Southeast. Competitors claimed we couldn't compete in the Midwest or Southwest without additional certifications. This forced us to spend even more money on testing to get the code reports required for those regions. After that, we hit another barrier: To expand further West, we needed an international building code certification. Again, we spent thousands of dollars on testing to earn that certification. All in all, we invested hundreds of thousands of dollars during this time. Still, eventually, we obtained the necessary approvals, and our competitors could no longer use those tactics against us.

The entire process—from dealing with the pyrite issue to navigating building code hurdles—felt like a series of near-death experiences for our business. But looking back, I see how those challenges strengthened our small company's resilience. I learned the importance of persistence, faith, and trusting God not as an escape but as a resource amid struggle. When faced with these problems, our focus wasn't on finding a way around them but on pushing through, knowing that God's strength would carry us.

WATER INTRUSION

Near-death experience number two was water intrusion, a challenge that hit almost exclusively residential homes, which was the majority of our work at the time. It became a massive problem for the EIFS industry, especially in the Southeast. Water would get trapped behind the walls, causing the substrate to rot, affecting hundreds of our homes over four or five years.

Most of our competitors were caught up in a class action lawsuit because of it, which shows just how widespread and serious the issue was. Master Wall was still small and relatively unnoticed, so we weren't pulled into the class action lawsuit. Looking back, I'm not sure if that was a blessing or a curse. Those companies were given a fixed settlement amount, allowing them to forecast and budget for the damage. Meanwhile, we dealt with each lawsuit on a case-by-case basis. We'd get calls from insurance companies coming after us, filing lawsuits one after another. We handled dozens and dozens of these cases through mediation.

This was unbelievably stressful, and I took it upon myself to handle the mediations. Week after week, I sat down with attorneys and insurance representatives to negotiate. It was exhausting and incredibly discouraging. The usual outcome involved agreeing to strip off the entire exterior of a home and replace it with something else—sometimes lap siding, sometimes hard coat stucco, and occasionally even brick. We were responsible not just for the strip-off but for installing the new system, too. The insurance companies typically covered part of it, but with a $10,000 deductible per job, it was still costing us a significant amount.

The situation became so severe that our original liability insurance company out of Pennsylvania went bankrupt, leaving us without coverage. By law, the Georgia Insurance Commissioner had to pick up our liability insurance since we were a Georgia corporation. They stepped in, but after a few months of realizing just how costly this could be for them, they came to us with an unusual offer, asking if they could buy us out of the policy they were responsible for. Things were so bad by then that I hired a bankruptcy attorney to explore our options. We were torn between accepting the buyout or filing for bankruptcy. Ultimately, we decided to take the buyout. It was a six-figure sum, and I felt it was a decent deal at the time.

The mediation process continued once they bought us out, but something interesting happened. The lawsuits stopped almost immediately once the insurance companies knew the Georgia Insurance Commissioner had given us that money. It was like a light switch flipped. I realized then that their goal wasn't to put us out of business—they just wanted every dollar we had. Once that money ran dry, the legal battles disappeared. It was surreal because these lawsuits and mediations had consumed years of my life. From the mid-'90s, when our liability insurance cost us around $8,000 annually, to the early 2000s, that cost had skyrocketed to over $400,000 a year.

Our financial situation grew so grim that we made a strategic move that I've partially regretted. We decided to initiate a preferred stock sale, offering shares to interested employees and bringing in an outside investor. As you might know, the idea behind preferred stock is to raise capital by selling shares that the buyer holds for a predetermined period, usually between one and five years. The funds generated from this sale were crucial at the time, allowing us to reinvest in the company.

After five years, we faced a critical decision: either buy back the stock or let it convert to common stock. Unfortunately, we couldn't afford to repurchase all the shares. While we managed to buy back as much as possible, the outside investor, who held a significant portion, kept his stake. When his preferred stock converted to common stock, it brought about complications. This investor, known for being tough and frugal, became actively involved in the company, even joining the board of directors. His involvement introduced a degree of tension that lingered for years, and it was only recently that we could buy back these shares.

Still, we managed to survive and keep moving forward. In the end, the moisture intrusion issue pushed our industry to be creative. We created what we call an EIFS Drainage System, which lets moisture escape if it gets behind our wall system. As a result, we have a much better system.

"QUIT WHILE YOU STILL CAN"

Unfortunately, tough days were still ahead. Once we overcame the water intrusion ordeal, we reconnected with a national consulting firm we had worked with in the late '90s. They would check in occasionally, but in 2001, they sent in one of their lead consultants to review our financials and see how we were doing. He took our financial records for the past few years, spent one night analyzing them, and returned with charts and notes that he plastered all over our conference room walls the next morning.

His message was blunt and devastating: "Do you want to come in for a belly landing or crash nose-first?" were his first words. I knew right away this news wasn't going to be pretty. Sure enough, over the next two hours, he detailed point by point how our business would never survive. In retrospect, I can't blame him. Our numbers weren't great, and from his vantage point, as an expert at a nationally recognized consulting firm, 99 percent of entrepreneurs in our situation probably *wouldn't* make it.

Our expenses grew faster than our sales because of rising insurance costs and other similar factors. Additionally, our receivables were aging out, which is fairly typical for a construction-related business, though most people might not realize that. In construction, it's common for clients not to pay their bills on time, so receivables tend to age out. When this consultant saw that our payments weren't coming in on time, rather than factoring in the nature of our industry, he concluded we didn't stand much chance of surviving.

Even though I understood these factors and didn't feel he was seeing the full perspective, his words still carried tremendous weight. Sometimes, the fear of the unknown eats at you the most. Amid random lawsuits and now some "expert" saying our company wouldn't survive, it was tough to know what to think. Maybe this guy was right. Maybe we shouldn't be in business. Perhaps I was just foolish and naïve, plunging ahead like a fool when it was only a matter of time before the guillotine would fall. *Quit while you still can*, I thought—but only momentarily.

Seconds later, I quickly pushed this negativity to the back of my mind and replaced it with my never-give-up mindset. I reminded myself that I didn't have any other options. I *had* to make this work. I resolved right then that I would prove this "expert" wrong. I'd survived too much to quit now.

Together with my amazing team, I doubled down, kept working, and somehow pulled through. Our determination carried us forward, and we managed to survive. We endured countless challenges along the way, including the aftermath of 9/11, which devastated the entire country and left everyone reeling for weeks. But we kept going even in the face of one obstacle after the next. We refused to give up, and against all odds, we made it through.

THE GREAT RECESSION

But just as life was getting good, Master Wall's third near-death experience hit in the form of the 2008 financial crisis.

I'm not sure whether most of the country realized just how devastating this time was for those in the construction industry—especially for companies like ours that weren't giants. This crisis was particularly devastating for the construction industry because it triggered a collapse in housing markets, leading to a sharp decline in demand for new construction projects. As credit markets froze, it became increasingly difficult for developers and homeowners to secure financing, causing many projects to be delayed or canceled.

Additionally, the widespread economic downturn resulted in reduced consumer spending and business investments, further shrinking the construction industry's pipeline of work and leading to widespread layoffs and bankruptcies within the sector. This financial hardship trickled down to companies like Master Wall, and for several years, we fought hard to survive and did everything possible to avoid laying off any of our employees. It was a tough commitment, but one we were determined to keep.

To get through it, everyone agreed to take pay cuts. Our hourly employees' hours were immediately cut. There just wasn't enough work to fill out a forty-hour week. Sales weren't there, and business dried up. As this did, so did the salaries. First, the management and executive team took a 10 percent pay cut. After a few weeks, we approached our hourly employees, telling them what we had done and asking them to accept a 5 percent cut.

Over time, the cuts deepened, with executives eventually facing a 40 percent reduction and hourly workers taking a 20 percent cut along with fewer hours. It was rough, but the reality was clear to everyone—this was happening everywhere, and the construction industry was hit especially hard. It wasn't like our people could go find work somewhere else. They wanted to keep their jobs, even if it meant barely scraping by.

We had to negotiate payment terms with vendors, pushing them out as far as they would allow. If we had thirty-day terms, we'd ask for forty-five days, then sixty days. Some vendors agreed and some didn't, forcing us to switch suppliers at times. We cut costs wherever possible—reducing everything from utility bills to insurance premiums. We scrutinized every expense, trying to find better deals on anything we purchased, from heating and power bills to health insurance through Blue Cross Blue Shield. Just to hang on to what we had, we didn't replace employees who left. Every move was about survival, and it wasn't easy.

We even explored some risky financing options beyond traditional banks. We contacted independent individuals for funding, a desperate but necessary move to keep our banking relationships intact. Even with those efforts, it was brutal. Starting in 2008, we lost a significant amount of money. I saw the impact not just on our company but across the entire industry. When we joined EIMA in 2018, I could see how badly the industry was affected by the Great Recession. Up until then, I didn't have access to those numbers. It took us and the entire industry six long years to recover. It wasn't until 2014 that our sales returned to 2008 levels.

Again, these were really dark times. Somehow, we made it through. To me, these were spiritual battles because, looking back, the numbers didn't add up, yet we still managed to survive.

PUSHING FORWARD IN FAITH

In those near-death experiences, we pushed forward, completing our code reports, which cost us a couple of hundred thousand dollars, despite the immense financial strain. All of this happened while we struggled to manage rising liability insurance premiums, keep our staff employed, maintain positive attitudes, and prove the consultant wrong who said we wouldn't survive. Our mission remained clear: "To God be the glory."

Looking back, I can see how God used each near-death experience to make us stronger and bear some good fruit. For example, the pyrite challenge was a difficult period, but one positive outcome was that we developed a strong reputation among local homeowners, especially in the central and west Georgia areas. We consistently stood behind our product, responded quickly, and ensured that the problem was resolved.

In some cases, we even fixed homes two or three times over a span of ten to fifteen years. This commitment helped us build a solid reputation with homeowners and contractors, who were all considered our customers. Locally, we became known as a company that stands behind its products and is committed to being a good neighbor in the communities where it operates.

There are other moments when I realize that the pain of a temporary situation prepared us for a greater challenge to come. Back when we were focused on obtaining code reports from organizations like the Southern Building Code and the International Conference of Building Officials, all I could think about was how much of a pain this was. Fast-forward a few years, and I recognized how God used that difficult time to prepare us for the 2008 financial crisis.

Even though these code reports took years to acquire, they allowed us to secure numerous commercial projects, including larger, multistory buildings. As a result, when the financial crisis hit, these commercial projects helped keep us afloat.

Despite our financial stress, we knew these code reports were important, and they started paying off just before the Great Recession hit. These efforts allowed us to continue building our reputation in the industry. Reflecting now, I am amazed at how God gave me the faith to believe we could persevere. I'm deeply grateful for the team members who weathered those storms with us, holding on with the confidence that we could make it through.

The reality is that building something meaningful requires a price. Some may ask why anyone would want to endure five, ten, or even fifteen years of hardship. My answer lies in my unwavering commitment. I didn't see any other option. We were going to make this work, one way or another. Yes, filing for bankruptcy might have been a legal escape route, but it would have left a stain on our reputation and taken years to recover from. So we decided to keep on fighting with God's help.

Looking back, I had friends and colleagues in the business world who chose easier paths when faced with adversity. They quit, found new opportunities, or simply couldn't push through. But for me, there was never a question of quitting. Our company culture was shaped by these struggles—getting knocked down and getting back up became who we are.

Some smaller competitors didn't survive those early days, especially in the Atlanta area. They were doing well and then vanished. It's a tough realization, but it solidified the mindset that resilience is essential. If someone reading this is on the verge of giving up, the difference between quitting and pressing on often boils down to faith and resilience. If I hadn't believed in 1987, 1988, and 1995 that I was supposed to be doing this, I wouldn't have had the faith to hold on. These challenges, in hindsight, always grew us, made us tougher, and improved our business. The adversity pushed us to refine our systems and innovate. Today, we have a better product because of what we endured, and my faith has increased.

I came to understand that God never promised to shield us from difficulties but that He walks with us through them. This realization transformed how I viewed adversity. It was no longer something to fear or avoid, but a necessary part of my journey that God would help me endure. Whether facing personal struggles, professional setbacks, or unforeseen crises, I found solace in the belief that I was not alone. This faith provided a sense of peace and purpose, even amid chaos, reminding me that every trial was an opportunity to trust God more deeply.

Knowing that God was with me gave me the strength to keep going when circumstances seemed insurmountable. I learned to rely on His guidance and timing, understanding that even the hardest moments had a purpose beyond what I could see at the time. This perspective allowed me to face each day with renewed hope and determination, confident that God was working all things together for good. My faith not only sustained me through tough times but also deepened as I witnessed God's faithfulness in every season of my life.

GUARD AGAINST DISTRACTION AND WORRY

If you're going through a near-death experience in your company, it's important not to give in to the threat of worry. Giving in will paralyze you.

Thankfully, I've never been one to let worry take over. I don't know if it's because I've learned to compartmentalize it or if I've just developed the ability to block it out, but I'm not a worrier, and hopefully I never will be. I'm more of a thinker, and while some might confuse that with worrying, it's not the same thing. I believe you must face challenges head-on and trust that you can find a way through them. I see problems as a challenge. I try to find a way through the problem, not worry or fret about the problem.

My journey with Master Wall is not that rare. Almost every company that has been around for more than a decade has had its share of tough times. Mine might have been more extreme, but I believe every company hits these near-death experiences to some degree. Sure, if you start with a huge pile of cash or have significant investors, you can avoid a lot of the hurdles. But that wasn't my situation, and I suspect it's not yours either.

When you're building something from the ground up, you are on this perpetual learning journey. There are hurdles that are just a part of the process. For example, I didn't have assets or a financial cushion to deal with things before they happened. Besides, I'd never run a business before—just a plant, a manufacturing facility. That's a different beast altogether, where you're not necessarily dealing with paying bills, collecting money, or handling the banking side of things. So, while my journey might seem extreme, I think these challenges are inevitable when you start with very little.

If you're worried about where your company is at, the first thing I'd tell you is to be absolutely sure this is what you want to do. Go back to what Simon Sinek says and start with your WHY. Keep focused on why you're doing what you do. As Sinek writes, "All organizations start with WHY, but only the great ones keep their WHY clear year after year."[17] They aren't easily distracted.

Once you start, you must keep your eye on the goal and not let worry get in the way. Have faith that it's the right thing to do and keep pushing forward, but make sure it's truly your path before you commit. That's crucial. Knowing why you're in it and coming back to that reason, especially when things get tough, is what keeps you going.

Is it hard to remain focused when you feel like your business is one heartbeat away from death? Absolutely. Staying focused in the middle of the mess didn't come naturally to me; it's something I've

---

17 Simon Sinek, *Start with Why: How Great Leaders Inspire Everyone to Take Action* (New York: Portfolio, 2009), 224.

had to learn over time. Like many, I am easily distracted. As Pastor John Mark Comer writes, "Western culture is arguably built around the denial of death through the coping mechanism of distraction."[18]

Maybe that's why God decided I needed these hardships—to keep me focused. Distraction has been and will always be a battle. I've got a note on my screen that says, "Distraction is the enemy of greatness." Little crises always emerge or small fires need to be put out. However, if I let worry and negativity consume me, I'll lose focus; this is something I can't afford to do, and neither can you.

THE VALUE OF HARD TIMES

It's been said that life is moving from one crisis to another with brief interludes in between. I wish the peaceful times lasted longer, but that's not how life works. Unfortunately, our current culture tends to lack patience for hard times—people switch jobs, quit when it's tough, or end marriages too quickly. But we often miss that true growth comes through enduring and persevering. Understanding this helps me stay prepared and resilient. Yes, there will always be challenges, but there will also be breakthroughs. And in those moments, I should give all the glory to God.

When I first started Master Wall, I expected a few rough years. But I expected things would level out and get easier. In some ways, they did. But with higher peaks came even lower valleys. In the beginning, it was hand-to-mouth survival—finding someone willing to buy our product just to keep the lights on. Later, the stakes were higher, but so was the level of resources at our disposal.

18 John Mark Comer, *Practicing the Way: Be with Jesus. Become like Him. Do as He Did.* (New York: WaterBrook 2024), 84.

Through every valley, the team watched me closely. My reaction to setbacks was critical. When I didn't fold and complain, neither did they. Instead, we all just got to work. I realized that if I just showed a little confidence and determination, the team would follow. This is what leadership is all about. It's setting the pace and instilling belief in the people who look to you.

The hardest part was balancing it all—especially at home. My wife bore the brunt of the stress. While I maintained a composed front at work, I was transparent with her about my fears. It wasn't easy for her, especially in the early years when I came home overwhelmed, uncertain, and stressed about being broke financially. But over time, she developed the same confidence I had. After watching us survive crisis after crisis, she began to trust that we'd always find a way through.

While I don't like hard times, they teach me lessons I wouldn't otherwise learn. It's that old saying that what doesn't kill you truly makes you stronger. You understand that success isn't a straight path; it's filled with ups and downs.

I've found that the ultimate purpose of hard times is to build my faith, increase my character, and strengthen my hope. The Apostle Paul said in Romans 5:3–4 (Christian Standard Bible [CSB]), "But we also boast in our afflictions, because we know that affliction produces endurance, endurance produces proven character, and proven character produces hope." They are refining moments. Our struggles don't disappear when we have faith. Rather, faith helps us navigate our struggles.

CHAPTER 4

Make Decisions for the Right Reasons

GOD SHOULD BE A RESOURCE IN THE STRUGGLE, NOT A WAY AROUND IT.

—GRADY NUTT

If you are a leader facing your own set of "near-death experiences," I guarantee you'll have to make some tough decisions. Decisions where you don't have all the facts, decisions that go against the thinking of some of your core leaders, and decisions that are made simply because they best align with your personal value structure.

One key benefit of being a majority stockholder is the ability to make executive decisions when necessary. After going through the experience of buying out the original investors, I learned a valuable lesson: You never want to be in a position where you own less than 51 percent of the company if you are the founder or one of the main stockholders involved. Maintaining a controlling interest allows you to steer the ship when needed most, and I wouldn't want to risk losing that leverage.

Although I've rarely had to exercise this authority, I've always appreciated the fact that, as the founder of Master Wall, I have that option. The buck stops with me. Yes, I take advice. Yes, I lean on others for support. In fact, most of the major and important decisions we make are not made in isolation but involve a group of people—ranging from a few to several individuals—to ensure a thoughtful and collaborative process. But at the end of the day, I am the one who must make the tough calls.

I must decide what is right.

MY CORE VALUES SHAPE MY DECISIONS

It's no secret that my faith plays an integral role in shaping my value structure, which in turn informs every decision I make, both personally and in business. I don't believe in compartmentalizing my life into separate categories where faith only applies to personal relationships, while business operates under a different set of rules.

God is part of my decision-making process. I agree with the founder of Texon LP, Terry Looper, that "God has a sacred pace all His own for the decisions of our lives, and every one of us needs His Holy Spirit to be able to discern it. In that sacred pace—in God's sovereign timing—His Spirit leads us to a sacred place: the center of God's will. Our part is to wait on the Lord with our eyes, ears, and hearts wide open."[19]

Because I'm anchored in faith, it becomes the foundation for everything—from the way I interact with people to how I approach difficult ethical decisions. I believe strongly that there is always only

---

19 Looper, *Sacred Pace*, 34.

one option, and that is to do the right thing, even when it's not the easiest or most profitable choice in the short term.

When my children were still in school, the two phrases I'd tell them every morning before they headed out the door were to "be like Jesus" and "do the right thing." They've heard those phrases hundreds of times. Doing the right thing is often tough. It takes a lot of courage and mental discipline.

The values that guide my personal life and family are the same ones that guide Master Wall. At Master Wall, faith informs the principles of integrity, honesty, and fairness that we try to live by, and those principles have become deeply embedded in our corporate culture. These values shape the way we conduct business on every level. In chapter 1, I shared the five core values of Master Wall's mission statement. These include

- manufacturing the highest quality EIFS and related products (coatings, adhesives, etc.) available in the market;
- being the service leader of our industry in the region and areas where we market our products;
- being respected in our industry because of honesty and integrity within our ranks;
- encouraging our employees to set the highest standards possible for their careers and personal lives, and compensating all employees well; and
- seeking God's guidance in all decisions and giving Him glory for any results.

Each of these core values impacts my decision-making process.

Why manufacture the highest-quality EIFS product? Because you can't enter a market and expect to succeed with an inferior product. It doesn't make sense.

You must aim to make the best product possible, preferably better than your competitors. After working for Dryvit System for seven years and before starting Master Wall, I had a clear understanding of what it took to produce high-quality products. From day one, we knew we couldn't afford to be anything less than the best if we wanted to compete.

One of my original stockholders, Billy Joe Donaldson, preached quality regularly. Being a plasterer by trade, he knew what quality felt like when applying the product. I spent so much time learning from him and others.

When I was hired by Dryvit in 1980, I knew nothing about the product, so that first year was dedicated to learning. The other major competitors at the time had roots in Dryvit too, so I knew the level of quality that was expected. It took a few years to feel like I had become an expert, especially once we started developing our own formulas at Master Wall. It wasn't easy, but we worked on refining our products for two or three years and have continued improving them since then.

Why strive to be the "service leader of our industry" when settling for something less would have been simpler? This ties back to quality. If another company can deliver in a week or two, we needed to at least match that, if not do better.

In the early days, we could get products to local contractors in two or three days, which gave us a huge advantage. Bigger manufacturers were slower because they sold through distributors, but we sold directly to contractors. That allowed us to offer better service right from the start, and our customers noticed the difference.

Quality service starts with having a great attitude and delivering high performance. In the construction industry, people don't mince words. If someone's not delivering, you'll hear about it quickly. I've had customers walk into my office to complain if our staff didn't greet them properly. So, our team understands how critical it is to stay on top of customer service, and they're usually all over it when a customer walks in.

Why focus on the core value of integrity? Because I operate in an industry where people often think, "business is business." They think you can operate one way at home and another way on the job site. But to me, business integrity is nonnegotiable. I've had vendors make promises they couldn't keep just to win our business, and that's not how we operate.

For example, early on, some of our competitors claimed their products were self-cleaning, which wasn't true. Over time, customers saw the reality and lost trust. So at Master Wall, we never made exaggerated claims about our products because we value honesty. What we promised was what we delivered.

The great thing is that when you tell the truth, you don't have to worry about keeping track of lies or changing your story! There's freedom that allows you to focus on what's important without the burden of deception weighing you down.

Why shoot for the core value of high standards for our employees? I see this as playing the long game. If you want long-term employees—and I do—you must care about their development; we send them to seminars and make continuous education available as well as other additional training. I love people, and I want them to succeed, so investing in their growth is crucial. Employees who know you genuinely care about their well-being and career development become more loyal. And that loyalty works both ways. You can't lead people without loving them.

Many of our employees have been with us for over twenty years, which is rare in this industry. In Lithonia, for example, I can name several who have been with us for over ten, fifteen, or even twenty-five years. That longevity comes from investing in our team. We believe in rewarding exceptional work through compensation, bonuses, and opportunities for growth. We celebrate employee anniversaries every five years of their service at our annual Christmas parties that are held separately at each location. In 2024, we actually celebrated the thirty-five-year anniversary of our longest-serving team member, Wendy Long.

Why seek God's guidance and aim to give Him glory? To me, this is the glue that holds everything together. It's the foundation of everything we do.

MISSION STATEMENT

TO SEEK GOD'S GUIDANCE IN ALL DECISIONS AND GIVE HIM GLORY FOR ANY RESULTS.

- TO MANUFACTURE THE HIGHEST QUALITY EIFS AND RELATED PRODUCTS (COATING, ADHESIVES, ETC.) AVAILABLE IN THE MARKET.
- TO BE THE SERVICE LEADER OF OUR INDUSTRY IN THE REGION AND AREAS THAT WE MARKET OUR PRODUCTS.
- TO BE RESPECTED IN OUR INDUSTRY BECAUSE OF HONESTY AND INTEGRITY WITHIN OUR RANKS.
- TO ENCOURAGE OUR EMPLOYEES TO SET THE HIGHEST STANDARDS POSSIBLE FOR THEIR CAREERS AND THEIR PERSONAL LIVES BY SUPPORTING THEM THROUGH EDUCATION, TRAINING, AND SHARING ANY GOD-GIVEN WISDOM WE MAY OBTAIN. TO COMPENSATE ALL EMPLOYEES IN SUCH A WAY THAT THEY CAN SUPPORT THEMSELVES AND THEIR FAMILIES IN A COMFORTABLE MANNER.

Master Wall COO and Senior Executive Vice President Mike Irving helped me see how these five values fit together several years ago. As you can see from this picture, the seeking God and glorifying Him value is set apart from the rest. Without this one, I believe the other core values fall apart. I believe that everything we achieve comes from His blessings, and we make it a point to acknowledge that as a team.

Not everyone outside our company appreciates this value. In fact, I had an attorney tell me we should remove this core value from the list. She said it was too exclusive. It goes back to the whole "keep topics like religion and politics in the home" bit. Sure, it's OK to believe in God. But it's wrong to think He has an opinion on how one should run a business.

But that's not and it will never be the way I look at things. To me, my faith should inform every decision I make, big or small. Work was one of God's first commands, so work and faith are intertwined. When you acknowledge that, everything becomes more meaningful. It's very important that I live out my faith in the way I do business, treat my employees, and serve my customers.

HIRE FOR THE RIGHT REASONS

After you set your core values, the key is to *never* compromise.

"How does compromise start?" Carey Nieuwhof asks. "Sometimes it begins intentionally. You know you're cheating. You know you're lying. You took the bait. But often, compromise doesn't begin that way. It happens more subtly."[20] In the Casting Crowns song "Slow Fade," the lyrics say "People never crumble in a day, it's a slow fade … when black and white have turned to grey."[21] This is where many leaders fall off the rails. To them, their core values evolve based on the circumstances. Sure, they have a general idea of right and wrong ways to run a business, but they'll bend their ideals if enough cash and opportunity come their way.

---

20 Carey Nieuwhof, *Didn't See It Coming: Overcoming the Seven Greatest Challenges That No One Expects and Everyone Experiences* (New York: WaterBrook, 2018), 43.

21 John Mark Hall, "Slow Fade," Casting Crowns, Be Essential Songs, 2007, https://www.wovenbywords.com/2009/10/slow-fade-by-casting-crowns.html.

At Master Wall, we've had many opportunities to compromise our values, but we've always stood firm in our commitment to doing things the right way, even when it costs us. One of the most frequent challenges we face is dealing with unethical practices in the construction industry. Shortcuts and shady deals are common in this space, and it's not unusual to encounter individuals who want to do business in a way that conflicts with our values. One of the main reasons for the near-death experience of water intrusion was contractors cutting corners and not installing the system properly.

In some situations, highly valued salespeople from competitors have approached us and offered to join our team. But we knew they had taken money under the table in the past. Maybe they brought a job lead to a contractor and received a kickback in exchange for choosing their product. They allowed their values to be governed by their wallet. While this type of behavior is unethical, in the past it was common practice.

When we become aware that someone has engaged in these practices, we decide not to hire them, no matter how much they might bring to the company in terms of sales. Early on, we made the mistake of giving a few people a second chance, thinking they had changed. But after a couple of years, we found out they were still operating the same way, and we had to let them go. It was a tough lesson but one that reinforced our commitment to staying true to our values.

Another example is in how we handle credit decisions. In this industry, many contractors promise to pay on time but then fail to meet their obligations. You must be cautious about who you extend credit to, and sometimes, that means making hard choices that could result in losing customers and a sale.

I've seen cases where customers owe us tens of thousands of dollars and are slow paying or not paying at all, yet I find out through social media that they're off on a European ski vacation or buying a new boat. That's a clear sign that their priorities are misaligned. Over the years, we have evolved to use distributors to sell our products. They are more professional and financially stronger businesses. Although we originally had to sell to contractors directly, we evolved to distribution as fast as we could.

Cutting customers or team members is never easy, but it's a decision we have to make to protect the company. While we may lose some business that way, it's necessary to ensure we're not constantly chasing payments from people who are dishonest. These ethical challenges used to arise almost daily until we became better at choosing who were reliable partners to extend credit to.

Each time, these challenges remind me of how my faith and values intersect with the practical realities of running a business. Whether it's deciding not to hire someone with a questionable past, turning down unethical business deals, or adjusting how we collect payments, I'm always guided by the principle that there's no separation between the values that guide my personal life and those that guide my professional life.

STICK TO YOUR VALUES

Sometimes, you have to make decisions that are controversial but are in alignment with your established values.

I am generally very cautious about getting involved in social or political issues as a company. While I have strong personal views on many matters, I've made it a point not to impose those views on Master Wall or use the company as a platform to push political agendas. We are not publicly political, even though I am personally very politically engaged. I believe it's important to maintain that separation of business and political and social issues.

That said, several years ago, during the Colin Kaepernick controversy, in which he kneeled during the National Anthem as a protest, I decided to make a policy that Master Wall would no longer use merchandise from Nike—which was Kaepernick's sponsor.

While I understand the importance of free speech in a free country, Nike's decision to keep Kaepernick's contract in place really bothered me. My employees know I value patriotism deeply. That being said, I did not want anyone on our team to think I condoned Kaepernick's or Nike's actions. After several months of observing the controversy, I called our marketing department and told them not to buy any more Nike products. I didn't want to see the Nike swoosh on anything related to Master Wall.

At the time, I felt this was the right decision for us because it aligned with my patriotic values. When I shared this with our leadership team and managers, the feedback was overwhelmingly positive. It was such a heated issue that nearly everyone was on board with the decision, and I'm confident that it was the right move for us, given the circumstances. This was not a called-for boycott. I may personally boycott some products or companies, but I would not call for or demand a boycott.

This experience gave me a valuable reminder that sticking to your values is crucial because it provides a consistent framework for decision-making and guides your actions, especially during challenging or uncertain times. When you stay true to your core principles, you build integrity and earn the trust of those around you, as people can rely on your predictability and honesty.

Values act as a moral compass, helping you navigate complex situations without compromising what matters most. Moreover, living by your values brings a sense of fulfillment and purpose, reinforcing your sense of self and making it easier to resist external pressures or temptations that might lead you astray. Ultimately, your values are the foundation of your character, shaping not just your personal choices but also the legacy you leave behind.

"Unfortunately," as author Gino Wickman writes, "most organizations have not defined their core values, and the resultant lack of clarity hinders their growth. When your people don't embrace your core values, their actions hurt your cause more than help it. By not defining what your values are, you have no way of knowing who believes in them and who doesn't."[22]

I'll make decisions around certain values, like patriotism, but when it comes to political opinions, I keep those separate from the business as much as possible.

MAKE THE TOUGH CALLS

Leaders frequently must make decisions when they don't have all the facts. Over the years, Master Wall has made several acquisitions that have expanded the business and brought in valuable assets, though they haven't been without their challenges. One of our first acquisitions was in Florida, where we purchased a store location called Just Right Supply, located just outside of Destin in Fort Walton.

This acquisition became part of a new entity we created called Creative Wall Products, which serves as our distributor in certain regions. However, not long after the purchase, we discovered that

---

22 Gino Wickman, *Traction: Get a Grip on Your Business* (Dallas: BenBella Books, 2012), 35.

some of the employees who came with the acquisition were stealing from us. There wasn't much oversight initially, which allowed the theft to go unnoticed.

Once we uncovered the issue, we had to go through the difficult process of restaffing the business. We've since relocated that operation multiple times, trying to find the right fit. It's been a journey, but we finally found a location on the other side of Destin, closer to Panama City, that works well for us. We've been operating there successfully for about seven or eight years now with a small but great staff.

We've also made other acquisitions, including a company in Texas called Rydar, which was based in Sealy. This acquisition eventually led to our Brookshire location. When we acquired Rydar, we had to renegotiate a lease and move the operations from Sealy to Brookshire, which was a significant undertaking. However, we gained a few excellent employees out of that deal who are still with us today, and they have been a valuable addition to our business. Rydar was a manufacturing company that was actually a competitor of ours, though much smaller. Acquiring them allowed us to strengthen our position in the Texas market.

In Georgia, we made another acquisition for Creative Wall Products. We purchased a storefront from General Shale in Marietta, Georgia. General Shale was a competitor selling another product in our industry. That acquisition also came with some outstanding employees, proving to be a solid investment for us. Additionally, a couple of years ago, we purchased a company called Universal Templates, which was based in New Hampshire. We relocated their operations down to Columbus and integrated them into our business structure. Each of these acquisitions has brought its own set of benefits and challenges, but overall, they have helped grow Master Wall in meaningful ways.

I had to make a series of tough decisions in each of these examples without having all the facts. I had to acquire, hire, and fire certain individuals all in a relatively short amount of time. It's moments like this where I felt my values put to the test.

I tend to slow the process down when it comes to making tough or big decisions, especially when faced with the conflict of what might be a good business decision versus what feels like the right decision. Whenever we discussed these acquisitions with our finance team, they often advised against them. From a purely financial standpoint, it didn't make sense at the time to spend the money we did. But for me, it's not always about what looks good short term on paper. I would take my time, pray about the decision, and really make sure to do as much due diligence as possible in the time frame I had.

Ultimately, I would conclude that it was the right thing to do. In every case, those decisions have worked out. Not only have these moves been good for our growth, but we've also gained some incredible people along the way. Even though the financial side of things didn't always align, those executive decisions often made with input from our leadership team turned out to be beneficial, although sometimes painful in the short term.

SLOW DOWN FOR TOUGH DECISIONS

My decision-making process tends to vary depending on the complexity of the situation. Simpler decisions, I can make instinctively without much need for consultation. However, the bigger the decision, the more I rely on input from managers and executives, especially when it's going to affect them directly. It's important for me to hear their perspectives.

That said, once I've gathered enough input and heard all the sides, especially the negative ones, I'll eventually push those voices out and make the final decision. At a certain point, you must turn off the doubts and move forward with confidence, knowing you've considered everything.

One of the greatest decisions I ever made, even though it wasn't a great financial decision, was buying out one of Master Wall's original stockholders. At the time, we were down to just the two of us, holding equal shares in the company after we'd bought out the third. The problem was that we had very different approaches to running the business.

He often wanted to pull money out of the business at the end of the year, suggesting we pay ourselves dividends or bonuses for tax reasons. But in those early years, I was adamant that we needed to reinvest that money back into the business—for growth, equipment, and stability. This back-and-forth tension became a regular source of frustration for me.

I eventually realized that we couldn't continue like this, and I needed to buy him out. The buyout was an exorbitant amount of money (at the time), which made me pause, but in the end, I knew it was the only way forward. It took twelve years of monthly payments to complete the buyout, but it was worth it.

Around the same time, I also extricated myself from another business we had together, one where we were leasing buildings and properties. Again, while not unethical, his approach to business didn't align with the integrity I wanted to uphold. I had to make the tough call to separate from him, even though it wasn't easy, especially because our families were close and our children were friends. That decision took a lot of prayer and careful consideration, and it was more of a personal and family conversation than a company matter.

Another significant decision was dealing with the water intrusion issue I referenced in the previous chapter. This was a massive challenge for us, and when the Georgia Insurance Commissioner came in and offered to buy out our policy, it was a huge risk. But like the stockholder buyout, this was a decision that required a lot of faith and careful thought.

These decisions weren't just business matters. They involved family, faith, and a deep sense of what was right for the company and me personally.

THE RIPPLE EFFECT

During my decades at Master Wall, we've made many decisions, and one key way we do that is through our leadership servant meetings, which happen every two weeks. These meetings bring together our leaders from all over the country, and even though they're in different locations, they call in, and we spend about an hour—sometimes more—discussing what's happening in their areas of the company.

If something comes up that doesn't align with our mission statement, we stop and address it right then and there. We encourage our team to make decisions that align with what we stand for, which we emphasize every time we meet. It's not just a onetime thing; it's woven into our operations.

This happens in our day-to-day operations as well. If I hear about a decision that needs to be made, I might go straight to someone's office and remind them, "Hey, we need to make sure this aligns with what we believe here." Are we being transparent? It's become a natural part of how we handle things.

Honestly, it's hard *not* to be conscious of this process. I'm thinking about it all the time, and the people in the home office—well, we're always talking about it. It's part of the culture. My sons, especially, hear it from me constantly. Once again, you must love the people you are leading.

My older son, Steven, whom we promoted to corporate vice president, has embraced this thinking. Our COO even told him how much he admires the way he cares for people, which speaks volumes about his character. You wouldn't necessarily think he'd be that way based on his outward personality, but he's deeply empathetic and genuinely helpful to others.

This mindset has just evolved over time. It's in the conversations we have, and it's reflected in the way we do business. Our mission statement isn't just something on the wall—it's everywhere. It's in the conference room and the break room, and all over the office. It's impossible to miss. It's who we are and what we strive to be. It's also in our literature, on our website—it's ingrained in everything we do. What's especially rewarding is when I see the ripple effect and how this way of thinking becomes part of the culture.

For example, we had a team member at our Lithonia manufacturing facility who faced serious health challenges. He was a production employee working on the floor making products, but he lacked personal transportation and relied on public transit to get to work every day.

After one particularly severe illness that required hospitalization, he was released but was too weak to ride the bus or train. That's when our plant manager at the time, Greg Wright, stepped in. Greg picked him up from the hospital, took him home to his apartment, and even bought him food along the way to ensure he had something to eat while recovering. This team member didn't have family or support in the area, so we became his family. Greg continued to help, taking him to follow-up doctor appointments and making sure he had food and support during his healing process.

This example underscores the essence of servant leadership. Greg's actions weren't part of his job description; they came from a place of compassion and genuine care for the well-being of his team. He went above and beyond because, in our company, we understand that leadership isn't just about overseeing operations. It's about uplifting those we work alongside. In the words of David Jeremiah, "The training for leading is serving."

REMAIN POSITIVE

So, how do you create a culture of right decision-making that is linked to good core values?

A great place to start is by creating a positive environment. I've always believed that if you keep talking positive, if you keep focusing on the good, it starts to change the atmosphere. It's especially important for the sales guys, who thrive on positivity. It's essential for them to stay motivated and optimistic to sell.

Still, positivity is important for the *entire* team. That's why I've put up whiteboards in each plant and facility and called them the "Positive Boards." My team encourages everyone to write something uplifting on them. Some jot down scriptures, while others post inspirational quotes. In *The Power of Positive Thinking*, Norman Vincent Peale writes, "The words we speak have a direct and definite effect upon our thoughts. Thoughts create words, for words are the vehicles of ideas. But words also affect thoughts and help to condition if not to create attitudes."[23]

There's this one guy in our Lithonia facility who's been through a lot in his personal life—divorces and other challenges—and every time I visit the plant, he's written something new. It's always just a

23 Norman Vincent Peale, *The Power of Positive Thinking* (New York: Touchstone, 2003), 17.

simple three or four sentences, but it comes straight from his heart. I've even taken pictures of his messages because they're so original and deeply meaningful. He writes things like, "Love yourself" or "Reflect on the good times." It's remarkable how something so simple can have such an impact.

I'm a quote guy through and through, so I never have any trouble finding or using quotes. Over the years, I've made it a habit to share them regularly. For a couple of years, I even sent out what I called the "Weekly Positive" email. It started as something small, but eventually, it went out to about fifty people in our organization and a few outside our company—pretty much anyone with an email address, except for the guys working on the floor. My goal was simple: *to keep morale high and keep the positive energy flowing*. I've included a few examples of these emails at the back of the book.

I think those little moments of positivity are good for all of us. That's why I try to write about them, talk about them, and live them. I remind myself and others that we should love the people we manage. Granted, this is easier for some than others. Not everyone has the natural empathy to care deeply, but if we keep talking about it, we can make them more aware of how important it is. That's a big part of the culture I try to build here—keeping people conscious of how they treat others.

In an industry like construction, where people come from all sorts of backgrounds and different companies with varying values, building a culture that focuses on doing things for the right reasons can be challenging. But I believe that, at the very least, people know what we stand for. They may not always act the same when they walk out the door after dealing with us as a vendor or buying our product, but when they're here, they know what we believe in and behave accordingly.

It's no secret who we are and what we value, and that sets the tone for how we interact with everyone who crosses our path.

KEEP FOCUSED

Making decisions for the right reasons is not only about what feels right in the moment but also about the long-term impact those decisions will have on your life, your team, and your organization. It's easy to be swayed by short-term pressures, external opinions, or the allure of immediate gain. But true leadership is about standing firm in your values, even when it's hard, even when it's unpopular, and even when the outcome is uncertain.

Every leader will face moments of tough decision-making—moments where they must decide between what's expedient and what's right. When you face these times, let your core values be your anchor. Whether it's personal faith, integrity, a commitment to quality, or a dedication to fairness, your values should serve as the compass that guides your path. Don't waver in the face of opposition or uncertainty; instead, lean into the principles that define who you are and what you stand for.

Making decisions for the right reasons isn't just about avoiding mistakes or managing risk. It's about building something lasting—whether that's a business, a team, or a legacy. When you choose to prioritize integrity over convenience, quality over shortcuts, and people over profit, you create a culture that others will want to be a part of. You inspire loyalty, foster trust, and set a standard that will outlive any immediate challenges you face.

So, as you move forward in your leadership journey, don't just focus on the decisions you make—focus on the reasons behind them. Let your values guide you, let your faith steady you, and let your integrity define you. The decisions you make today will shape the future, and when they are made for the right reasons, they will lead you, your team, and your organization to success that is not only meaningful but also lasting.

CHAPTER 5

Notice Everyone's Strengths

WHATEVER YOU FOCUS UPON, INCREASES.
—ANDY ANDREWS

As your organization grows and you hire more employees, your approach to leadership must shift. It's imperative to remember that each team member plays a distinct role. They are not irreplaceable, but they are uniquely valuable. It's these differences that make an organization strong.

There is a passage in the Bible that I love. It's 1 Corinthians 12:12 (NKJV), which says, "For as the body is one and has many members, but all the members of that one body, being many, are one body, so also *is* Christ." The imagery is that some people are the hands and others are the feet, but we all play a role. We're all interconnected. Together, these differences complete the body. It's the same in business.

For example, engineers are often very detailed but not as empathetic, while salespeople are social butterflies but can't seem to manage their expenses. Customer service folks often strike a balance between being administrative and people-oriented, while those in research and development or quality control tend to be more solitary and focused on their work without much need for interaction. Despite these extremes, you need all of these types of people to build a good business, and I've learned over forty years of managing people to respect those differences.

True organizational success requires all kinds of people. Whether it's a basketball team, a church, or a business, you must respect everyone's strengths and differences. How do you find people with the right strengths and get them on your team? The key is to sit up and pay attention.

NOTICE PEOPLE'S STRENGTHS

One of my favorite books is *The Noticer* by Andy Andrews. As the narrative unfolds, an insightful, unassuming man named Jones shows up in people's lives when they're going through tough times, offering them something even more valuable than quick fixes: perspective. In one section, Jones writes, "In desperate times, much more than anything else, folks need perspective. For perspective brings calm. Calm leads to clear thinking. Clear thinking yields new ideas. And ideas produce the bloom … of an answer."[24]

Instead of solving people's problems directly, Jones helps them see things from a different angle. He believes that how we view our circumstances often determines the outcome. His gift is in observing people's situations and helping them discover their own strengths to create positive change. Throughout the book, Jones meets people

24 Andy Andrews, *The Noticer: Sometimes, All a Person Needs Is a Little Perspective* (Nashville: Thomas Nelson, 2009), 154.

dealing with all kinds of issues—financial struggles, broken relationships, or feeling lost in life.

He doesn't offer one-size-fits-all advice. Instead, he listens and tailors his wisdom to each person, helping them realize that their personal strengths and experiences can actually be their greatest tools. Whether it's encouraging someone to be more patient or step outside their comfort zone, or reminding them of their worth, Jones focuses on the power of embracing one's unique gifts. He shows that a small shift in perspective can make all the difference.

Jones highlights how noticing and appreciating what makes each person unique can lead to breakthrough moments, especially when it comes to working with others. Whether it's in a team, family, or community, our differences are what make us stronger. Instead of dividing us, our varied strengths can complete the bigger picture. Jones's wisdom reminds us that when we recognize and respect the individual gifts people bring, we can accomplish so much more together.

Ultimately, *The Noticer* is a powerful reminder that everyone has something valuable to offer, and it's often our differences that make us better. Whether in business, personal relationships, or life in general, learning to see and appreciate each person's strengths helps build a more connected and successful environment. It's all about perspective and finding the right fit for everyone.

I'm not someone who is big into personality tests, but like Jones, I do watch people closely. I notice what they say and don't say. I notice their body language. I notice who they connect with and who they don't. Based on my observations, gut instinct, and life experience, I tend to know if someone's strengths are a fit or not.

THE RIGHT SEATS ON THE BUS

In *Good to Great*, Jim Collins says great leaders "first got the right people on the bus, the wrong people off the bus, and the right people in the right seats—and then they figured out where to drive it."[25] From my experience, you know someone is in the wrong seat when both they and the organization are unhappy.

It's usually not just about poor performance—it's about that deep-seated sense of discomfort when things just aren't clicking. When people are in the wrong role, you can see it in how they approach their work. They might be frustrated, disengaged, or even resistant to change. The organization feels it too—there's a strain in workflow, communication, or results. In situations like that, it's often about figuring out where someone's strengths really lie and adjusting their role accordingly.

A lot of this comes down to understanding people's gifts and strengths. Take salespeople for example. Stereotypically speaking, individuals who are great at sales are terrible at details. They love engaging with people and personal interaction. They loathe the idea of sitting down at their computers to fill out an expense report. It drains the life out of them and makes them want to quit. Whenever I run into someone like this, I do my best to work with them. I deal with their weaknesses because their strengths are great.

On the flip side, there are times when it becomes clear that someone simply doesn't belong in the organization. When someone doesn't enjoy their job, and their performance suffers, it's often a sign they're not in the right seat—or maybe not even on the right bus. In those cases, it doesn't take long to figure out they're not trying to

25 Collins, *Good to Great*, 13.

fit in. At that point, it becomes about making a hard decision: *Do I reorganize them or let them go?*

KNOW YOUR STRENGTHS AS A LEADER

To understand the strengths of others, you must first recognize what you are and are not good at. I'm a big-picture guy. I have a clear sense of where an organization needs to go and what needs to be done, especially when it comes to setting a vision. This comes naturally to me, and it's a gift that has served me well—particularly in manufacturing.

When it comes to building a team, I sometimes take an unconventional approach. There have been times when I've seen someone who's really talented at something—whether in church or elsewhere—and I've thought, *We need to bring this person in*. Even if there wasn't a spot in the budget or an immediate need, I knew we could find a place for them. This can drive people in administration a little crazy, especially when they're trying to stick to the budget, but it has worked out well more often than not.

However, my weakness is not always knowing how to reach the end destination. I'm not great with the details or the "nuts and bolts" of making things happen. That's where I rely on people like our COO Mike Irving, our CFO Susan Ellis, and Sales Manager Grant Smithwick. They're the ones who figure out the steps, budget cuts, purchases, and logistics.

I'm a bit of a dreamer and can sometimes lack focus, so I need those detail-oriented people to make things work. Though I've never been diagnosed with ADHD, I'm pretty sure I have it based on how quickly I lose focus and move on to the next thing. My wife likes to remind me of that from time to time.

One of my pros, and cons, is that I'm generous to a fault. Again, this sometimes frustrates people on my team when I offer second chances or benefits that don't align with the bottom line. It's here I've done a bit of give and take. Sometimes, I've realized I need to scale back and be a bit more strategic. Other times, I've doubled down and encouraged those on my team to be more generous.

A great example is our CFO. She came from the oil industry, where everything is structured and following the budget is almost a rule of law. At first, I drove her crazy because our way of doing things was so different from what she was used to. I've learned a lot from her, but she also realized she needed to adapt.

For instance, early on, she made a few questionable hires. It was just a learning curve, and she had to learn more about who I was to understand the types of people that would fit in our organization. So, on Monday afternoons, we started meeting and discussing the decision-making process. I learned from her, and she learned from me. Now, she is one of the most valuable members of our team.

THE SPEED OF TRUST

One of the common mistakes I see leaders make is trying to get everyone in the right seat on the bus in one afternoon. They know where they want to take people and adopt a "my way or the highway" mentality. If those on their team don't perfectly align with their vision, they kick them off or move along to another organization that will let them lead the way they want to. These types of leaders think their way is the only way. Often, there are many different routes to a destination, and one of those routes may make a better trip.

I think of one church leader I worked with years ago. He was an incredible speaker with a fantastic background. He was actually part of the military operation in Somalia featured in the film *Black Hawk Down*—a real-life hero with leadership skills and a talent for communication. He spent over a year learning the ropes from our retiring pastor, and when he took over, the church initially grew under his leadership. People were drawn to his platform skills, and he had a natural gift for evangelism, which brought in a lot of new faces. But over time, it became clear that while he was a great communicator, he wasn't the right fit as a pastor.

In my opinion, he didn't have the pastor's heart that's needed to care for people in more personal, emotional ways. The crossover from the military to a local church community was tough. It wasn't his gift to be the type to visit people in the hospital or provide that comforting presence that many members needed. He was a tough, no-nonsense kind of guy. And while that worked well in certain settings, it was harmful in others.

Eventually, this disconnect started to create tension within the church. This leader had a lot of ideas about restructuring and changing things, particularly around how we managed our retirement center and assisted-living programs. As the months went on, people became uneasy with these changes.

It all came to a head when this leader decided to restructure how we handled our elder and deacon leadership roles. In a meeting, he gave us an ultimatum. He sent out an email with his resignation attached during the meeting, essentially saying, "If you don't agree to these changes, I'm out." It was a bold move, and it caught everyone off guard.

We were already frustrated with the direction things were going, so we accepted his resignation, which was not what he expected. What followed was months of division and struggle. The staff loved him, but many of the elders and deacons were tired of the constant changes and the friction it all caused. It was a tough time for the church, and it was painful to see how it divided people. I remember thinking how much I never wanted to be involved in that kind of conflict, but there I was, right in the middle of it.

At lunch one day, I sat down with this leader and had a heart-to-heart conversation. I handed him a copy of Stephen Covey's book *The Speed of Trust*—a gesture I'm not sure he fully appreciated. In this book, Covey writes, "The first job of a leader—at work or at home—is to inspire trust. It's to bring out the best in people by entrusting them with meaningful stewardships, and to create an environment in which high-trust interaction inspires creativity and possibility."[26]

This leader was a great individual with so much potential. He was just moving too fast for others to follow. Eventually, he left and started a new church.

After this leader left, our church brought in a pastor with a completely different approach. The new pastor is a people person through and through. He's great on the platform, but he also has a pastor's heart. He's the kind of person who can walk into a hospital room and make people feel cared for. He's likable and approachable, and he understands the importance of connecting with the congregation on a deeper level. Most importantly, he operates at a speed with which others can keep up.

DIFFERENT STRENGTHS OF THE FAMILY

As a dad with kids who work in my business, I've certainly noticed the different strengths that run through my kids. My oldest son, Steven, is now our corporate vice president. He presides over our Creative Wall stores and handles other product responsibilities as well.

---

26 Covey, *The Speed of Trust.*

Steven's personality is unstructured—he doesn't have the gift for administration or management—but he's exceptional with products and teaching about them. He's a great listener, which is a valuable gift, though he comes across with an alpha personality. Despite that, he has a lot of empathy for people. He started working with us at a very young age, probably around twelve or thirteen, helping after school by making product samples. He's been with us ever since, and though he's not a natural manager, he's found his place and is doing great work.

Then there's my daughter Natalie. She worked for the company for the first few years we were in Columbus. She started as a receptionist and helped with payables in the accounting department. People absolutely loved her—she has a very likable personality, a great phone voice, and made a perfect first impression when people came into the office. Natalie has since moved on to be an administrative assistant at the school her five children attend. She has a lot of great gifts, especially for communication and connection, and those were invaluable when she was with the company.

My middle son, Grant, is our national sales manager. He's the ultimate people person—he loves meeting people, socializing, and taking customers out for lunch or a round of golf (which, by the way, he's great at, though I don't play myself). His gift is in building relationships, which is crucial for his role. He thrives in situations where he can connect with customers and potential clients on a personal level. Grant's social nature and love for engaging with people make him a perfect fit for sales, and he truly enjoys what he does. He brings a lot of energy and enthusiasm to the team, and his ability to connect with people helps drive our business forward.

Finally, there's my youngest son, Stewart. He's our IT guy and has a degree in marketing. Stewart handles our website and all the technical aspects of the business. He's more of an introvert—definitely not a people person. He prefers to stay in his office and work quietly, focusing on the technical side of things. He's incredibly gifted when it comes to technology and marketing, and though he's not as social as Grant, he plays a critical role in our company. His attention to detail and technical expertise help keep everything running smoothly behind the scenes.

All four children have very different personalities, strengths, and gifts. They didn't always start in the right positions, but over time, we found the roles that suited them best, and now it all works well together. I know I am truly blessed to have my family with me every day, and there are always great reminders of why this is rewarding. But this one scene from an episode of *Landman* I was watching one evening nailed the very essence of why it is such a great privilege to work with my family. Owner, president, and general manager of the Dallas Cowboys, Jerry Jones, comes to talk to Monty Miller (Jon Hamm), who is on his death bed. Here is a transcript of what he says:

> My daughter, when I was in my thirties, went to school at Stanford. I couldn't stand it. She was so far from Arkansas. So, I'd think of reasons to make trips out there, try to come up with a little business or something. I'd go out there with her. I'd ... We had an old office, downtown Palo Alto. I ... Uh ... Jean goes to class with her. I said, "You know, I need to get some things going out here, if I'm gonna spend this kind of time." So I went over to Brentwood, about twenty or thirty miles from San Francisco. And I bought about twenty-five lots like I was gonna build twenty-five houses. Except I drilled four gas wells. And those four gas wells, in eighteen months, paid me enough money

for me to buy the Dallas Cowboys. Paying attention to my kids actually led me to getting involved in the passion of my life. And all along what I was trying to do was hang out near my daughter. Lot of things happen that you didn't have planned or don't have the strategy for. Now, I'm not saying I've done anything right, but I made my mind up a long time ago I was gonna work with my kids. And they're involved in everything. They're involved in my leasing, oil and gas, real estate. And so, when I got the Cowboys, I got it so that we could all work together. I thought I was doing it for them. But the one that got the most out of it was me. I just know it's not gonna be this time, but you're gonna be sitting here sometime in the future, laying here sometime in the future ... and this room's gonna be full of your business associates and the people you've worked with all your life. And more than likely, your children and family are gonna be there because they're your children and your family. But you could have 'em there because they're the people you spent your life with, you worked with, you fell down with, you got up with. Not just Thanksgiving and Christmas. That's who you want to be with. So when that time comes like this, it's a celebration of your life and you're not wishing you'd spent a little more time seeing a few more suns come up. That's the trick. That's the trick. 'Cause that's gonna be your glory. I'm pretty proud of them Cowboys. I'm pretty proud of ... the stuff we've done, and ... oil and gas. It pales in comparison to how proud I am to have lived my life working with my kids.[27]

27 "Landman Season 1, Episode 9 'WolfCamp' Transcript," TV Show Transcripts, March 14, 2025, https://tvshowtranscripts.ourboard.org/viewtopic.php?f=2391&t=72504.

As a dad, one of the smartest things I did early on was ensuring I wasn't directly managing my kids. I didn't want to mix family dynamics with management responsibilities, so I put Mike Irving, our COO, in charge of them. That decision has been one of the best I've ever made. It created a healthy separation between me as their father and me as their employer, which has been crucial for maintaining balance.

Then, there is my wife, Donnie. She came to work for the company in 2018 after leaving her role as an admissions director at a school. She's incredibly skilled in writing, grammar, and technology—areas where I'm lacking. I could not have written this book without her grammar skills. She's also one of the few people who can really hold me accountable, and I need that. Her gift for hospitality has been a tremendous asset to the company as well. She handles all the social events, like setting up lunches for customers and organizing our Christmas parties.

My hope is that the skills and strengths my family members have acquired over the years at Master Wall prove invaluable no matter where life takes them. They don't have to remain part of this business, but I've set up a succession plan if they choose to do so.

I write this recognizing that family businesses often fall apart because of the different personalities and dynamics within the family. According to the Harvard Business Review, 70 percent of family-run businesses fail or are sold before the second generation takes over.[28] I've seen it happen, and it can be tough if you don't know how to make it work. Each family has its own set of challenges, and it takes a lot of effort to respect each person's strengths and differences. If you don't have the ability to do that, things can quickly unravel. It's definitely

28 George Stalk Jr. and Henry Foley, "Avoid the Traps That Can Destroy Family Businesses," *Harvard Business Review*, January 2012, https://hbr.org/2012/01/avoid-the-traps-that-can-destroy-family-businesses.

not easy, but I've been fortunate to have a great team around me, made up of both family members and non-family members.

DIFFERENT STRENGTHS WITHIN THE ORGANIZATION

In addition to a great family, I'm also blessed with a strong team. Mike Irving, whom I've mentioned several times, has been with us for nearly thirty years. When I first hired him, I wasn't sure we could afford him, but I knew I needed him. He's taken on several roles over the years, from technical services to sales management, and now he's our COO. Mike is incredibly structured and organized, always planning months ahead. I've learned a lot from him, especially about discipline and budgeting. He's been a strong leader and is fully aligned with our company's mission, which is essential for our team.

Then there's Greg Wright, our operations manager, who's been with us for about twenty years. He's an engineer with a degree from Georgia Tech, and he has a real gift for details. Greg is passionate about safety and compliance, tackling EPA and OSHA regulations with enthusiasm—something not many people enjoy. While he's not as strong in the manufacturing processes, he excels in the legal and safety aspects of our operations. He's also incredibly empathetic, which makes him a great leader for our team.

Dennis Deppner, our technical services manager, is another long-time employee with over twenty years at the company. He's well-known in the industry for his customer service skills and technical knowledge, and has an architecture and engineering background, which makes him perfect for his role. Our customers love him, and he's fully committed to our mission. Dennis is quick to meet customer needs and has built a strong reputation for his responsiveness.

Debbie Wetherington worked with us for twelve years before retiring and going to work in her family business. She was my administrative assistant, handling my travel, customer service, and many other tasks. She was an all-star who could do anything. I first noticed her when she was my grandson's pre-K teacher.

Carolynn Nale is one of those people whose work ethic and personality caught my eye right away. My wife and I used to go to a restaurant in Harris County fairly often, and we'd sit at the bar, which was a great place to meet people and talk. Carolynn was the bartender, and after watching her work a couple of times, I was really impressed. She was fast, efficient, and people just loved her. I remember telling my wife, "This girl is phenomenal."

After a few visits, I told her that she'd be an all-star in customer service. It took a little while, but eventually, she agreed to join us, and she's been with the company for about five or six years now. She's been exactly what I expected—absolutely perfect for the role. Her husband even came to work for one of our other companies a couple of years later. Sometimes, you just know when you've found the right person for your team, and with Carolynn, we didn't even have a job opening at the time, but I knew we had to find a place for her. As it turned out, one of our other customer service employees retired shortly after she started, and it worked out perfectly.

Another person who's been crucial to our company is Wendy Long, our credit manager. I mentioned her previously as our longest-serving employee who isn't a family member. Wendy has done a lot of different things over the years, but she's been in credit management for about thirty of those years. What makes her so great at her job is that she despises dishonesty. In the construction business, you deal with a lot of people who can be less than straightforward, and Wendy's heard every excuse in the book. She'll tell me about her interactions with customers, and we joke that she could write a whole book on the various lies and excuses she's been told. Her ability to see through that nonsense has made her invaluable in collecting payments and managing credit. She's incredibly loyal, knows the business inside and out, and has been a real asset to us for decades.

Another key person in my career was Deborah Culpepper. Deborah worked with me back when I was at Dryvit, where she was my administrative assistant. Later on, I hired her part-time at Master Wall. She had needs within her family that led her to eventually take another job, but she continued to make color charts for me on the side. She would cut stucco blocks and glue them to the charts, and unfortunately, after doing that for a while, she developed carpal tunnel syndrome and had to have surgery. Even after that, she came back to work for us, helping out with payables. She was one of those people you could always rely on—hardworking and ethical, with a depth of character that made her stand out. She's still a close friend of my wife's, and though she's no longer with us, she left a lasting impression.

There's Sharon Brown, who has been with us for over twenty-five years. We hired her to become a colorist to match colors for us, which she knew very little about. She has become extremely good at this and basically was self-taught. In her twenty-five years of working at our Lithonia plant, she has been the only woman for most of the time. It made her strong, and she kind of became the "Plant Mom." Sharon has been a very loyal employee. She is going to retire soon and will be missed.

Jeff Muir is our plant manager in Payson, Utah, and is also responsible for sales for one of our largest distributors in the country. Our Utah plant supplies products for the entire western US market. Jeff calls himself our "stepchild" because he takes care of everything himself and doesn't have to interact with leadership and management. He does a great job for us and takes care of virtually *everything* on his own.

Leo Crowell joined us in 2004 as regional sales manager for the Midwest and part of the Southwest. Leo does not fly on airplanes. He drives everywhere to service his customers. After being with us for over ten years, he asked us to buy him an RV since he spent so much time driving. We thought he was joking, but he wasn't. Since we never bought him the RV, he continues to make those drives to service his customers. Leo has a great sense of humor that all of us love.

Mark Walker was with us over twenty years in our accounting department. He held the controller position and was with us through at least two of the near-death experiences I mentioned earlier in the book. Mark was loyal and stuck with us no matter how bad it got.

Then there's Mike King. I've known Mike for nearly forty years, and when we bought the Marietta location of General Shale and added it to our locations for Creative Wall Products, he was one of the main reasons we made the deal. Mike has a stellar reputation for running a distribution location. He's done it for his own business, and later for other companies after selling his business. We brought him in, and he's been an absolute jewel for us. He runs a great store, even though not everyone finds him easy to work with. He's extremely structured and tough, which can rub some people the wrong way. But Mike's an ex-Marine, and at seventy-five years old, he's still sharp, disciplined, and incredibly effective. His results speak for themselves, and that's why we value him so much.

THE KEY IS TO LOVE PEOPLE

The problem with so much self-help leadership material today is that the underlying motivation is based on a faulty foundation. It's not about doing the right thing because it's the right thing. It's about doing something (not the right thing) to manipulate people to do what you want them to do. I don't like that teaching because that's not the right thing to do. If you are going to lead, you must love those you want to lead.

Looking back, I'm so glad I had that painful experience in Phoenix several decades ago that motivated me to write down my core values. If I hadn't been shut out of that conference and had to make the long drive back across the country, I'm not sure I would have taken the time to value others as I do today. But that week changed everything. It motivated me to be a better leader and solidified what I believed.

I realized that if I wanted to make the right decisions when my business was thriving, I had to make the right decisions when my team was small and didn't get much respect. Even though I felt shut out, I was determined to open the door for others. I'd already experienced life at the other end of the spectrum. I'd seen how the culture at my previous company, Dryvit, was a dog-eat-dog environment, full of backstabbing and political maneuvering. Yes, they were successful, but I didn't want a business like that, even if it meant success.

I've always believed you've got to love the people you work with, especially if you're in charge of them. You've got to care about them, and they'll know if you don't. That's why, when you look at our mission statement, there's a whole section dedicated to how we want to treat our people. I've always loved people, and I've always liked taking care of them.

One criticism of me is that I'm sometimes too quick to hire people because it gives me the chance to help someone else, give them a job, provide benefits, and support them. The finance team has definitely given me some grief about that over the years, and I've had to dial it back because it's not always realistic. But that's who I am. I love taking care of people, and if I could, I'd hire twenty more just to feel like we're doing something good.

Be good to people, care for them, and show them a good way to live. Those have always been a few of my guiding principles. Today, I've got all kinds of people working for me, and I love that diversity. Our workforce includes multiple minorities, ethnicities, and religions.

I just love people, and I want our company's decision-making process to reflect that.

PRINCIPLES TO SHARE

As I reflect on forty-plus years of working with people, there are a few principles I'd share with a young leader over a cup of coffee.

First, I truly believe that most people want to do a good job. The key is getting them in the right place where their strengths can shine, even if they don't know what that is themselves. When you take the time to listen to them, observe them, and find that right fit, people will enjoy their work and perform well.

Second, you have to be a "noticer." Pay attention to people, listen to them, and understand what makes them tick. I've learned over the years that by noticing the small things—how people behave and how they respond to situations—you can figure out a lot about them and where they might fit best in the organization.

Lastly, love people. I've said it before, but it bears repeating. I love helping people, employing them, and taking care of them. That mindset has been a huge part of my success, and I believe it's crucial for anyone who wants to lead effectively. Being in a position where I can make decisions, take care of people, and help them find their path has been one of the most rewarding aspects of my job. Of course, there are challenges, and not every decision is easy, but when you lead with a genuine love for people, it makes a big difference.

When it comes to helping others recognize the strengths in their team members, the key is to be open and transparent about what you see. I've always been direct when I notice red flags or signs that something might not be working out with a new hire. For instance, when I see someone who has been hired, but it doesn't seem like they'll last, I'll talk to Mike or others about it and say, "I don't think this will end well." It's not always easy to explain exactly why, but it often comes down to things like a lack of openness and transparency. If someone isn't engaging or doesn't seem like they really want to be part of the team, that's a warning sign.

A lot of it comes down to gut instinct, but there are small behaviors that can be telling too. For example, if someone consistently avoids conversations, only gives one-word answers, or is always the first one out the door at the end of the day, those are signs that they might just be doing a job rather than being invested in the team. I use John Maxwell's phrase with managers: "Walk the halls slowly." That means making time every day to walk around the business, speak to everyone, and gauge their engagement. If someone gives you the cold shoulder or barely acknowledges you, that's a clue that something might be off.

It's important to stay approachable as a leader, even though some people may see the title of president or CEO and assume they can't relate to you. But I believe that if people take the time to communicate with me, they'll see I'm pretty relatable. You can tell a lot by these everyday interactions, and it helps in figuring out if someone is in the wrong role or if there are deeper issues at play.

In diverse settings, it's crucial to listen to others' views, respect their opinions, and keep the door open for dialogue, even when you disagree. I've often used the analogy of the body—eyes, hands, and feet—when responding to complaints about a team member who may not seem like a good fit.

I remind people to think about the individual's strengths and whether they're in the right place. Maybe they shouldn't be the hands but the feet, or the eyes instead of the mouth. The whole team is like a body, and each part has a unique role to play. It's about finding where each person fits best for the team's overall health.

CHAPTER 6

Remain True to Who You've Committed to Be

KEEPING IN TOUCH WITH GOD WON'T ELIMINATE YOUR PROBLEMS; IT WILL ONLY HELP YOU MANAGE THEM.

—UNKNOWN

This brings us to arguably the most important chapter in this book. After you've decided to lead with the right values and started putting those beliefs into practice, the key is longevity. *Can you remain committed to the person you've told yourself and others you will be?*

Remaining true to myself has been the guiding principle through everything I've undertaken. To me, commitment is sacred. Once I've dedicated myself to something, I don't back out and certainly don't quit. Instead, I establish my core values and follow them. These are not just words or ideals but the essence of who I am and what I believe. Throughout my decades-long journey to reach where I am today, that commitment to staying true to myself has been my foundation.

The essence of remaining true to yourself is knowing what you believe and habitually acting on that belief with consistency and determination. As James Clear writes, "Behavior that is incongruent with the self will not last."[29] Everything you do—whether it's following a mission statement or the personal mantra of never giving up—should be an extension of your beliefs. The problem is that it is really, really hard.

It's one thing to be committed for a week, but it's another thing to be committed to your values for a lifetime.

CONSISTENCY IS REALLY HARD

Christian author Daniel Henderson says, "The hardest thing about the Christian life is that it is so 'daily.'"[30] The same holds true in business and life. Sometimes the grind of life wears us down. We set clear goals, make a series of good decisions, and build a strong team. But then, something happens, and we fall off the rails. We stop being true to the person we've committed to be.

Part of the problem is we get tired. Fatigue, more than anything else, is the biggest threat to remaining true to myself. The exhaustion that comes from endless days, constant decisions, and relentless pressures is often overwhelming. When I'm tired, that's when I make my worst decisions. I've seen this pattern play out in my personal life as well as in business. It's during these moments of fatigue, when

29 James Clear, *Atomic Habits: An Easy & Proven Way to Build Good Habits & Break Bad Ones* (New York: Penguin Publishing Group, 2018), 32.

30 Daniel Henderson, "Finding Daily Renewal in the Lord Jesus Christ," Strategic Renewal, accessed November 4, 2024, https://www.strategicrenewal.com/finding-daily-renewal-in-the-lord-jesus-christ/.

I'm at my weakest, that my judgment wavers. Staying true to myself requires energy and clarity.

As a basketball coach for many years, I noticed this battle with fatigue both with myself and my players. Toward the end of the season was when we felt exhausted and were stretched to the max. But this was when we needed to be at our best because it was the playoffs.

Coaching at the playoffs.

As the coach, this wasn't any time to slack off. It was my time to muster what enthusiasm I had, deliver a pep talk, and keep my team encouraged at halftime. Yes, I was tired. Also, during the season I was running a growing business. The last few years, the schedule was so stressful that my immune system couldn't fight off the bronchitis that I was prone to get. I stayed sick for weeks but just kept going. I had to remember it was still important to be on top of my game, come up with fresh ideas, and keep our team committed to the core principles that shaped the way we played. As author Jon Gordon writes, "Distraction is the enemy of greatness."[31]

The same principle holds true in life and business, where distractions and pressures constantly threaten to pull us away from our principles. The temptation to chase quick success, the need to meet deadlines, and the desire to please others can blur the lines of commitment. When we're tired, these temptations feel even stronger, and it's easy to stray off course. That's why managing fatigue is so crucial. Whether it's taking time to rest, seeking advice, or simply reminding ourselves why we started, we must learn to recognize these vulnerable moments and find ways to recharge.

Ultimately, staying true to ourselves isn't a onetime decision. It's a continual process of aligning with our core beliefs, even when things get difficult.

THE VALUE OF COMPOUNDING GOOD HABITS

When people ask me how I avoid burning out, I tell them it's a mix of small, consistent habits that ground me. As Darren Hardy writes in *The Compound Effect*, "The secret to success was then, and is now, hard work, discipline, and good habits."[32] In this book, Hardy shares the story of "The Magic Penny" as follows:

31 Jon Gordon, "Distraction Is the Enemy of Greatness," X (formerly Twitter), November 14, 2023, https://x.com/JonGordon11/status/1724588774162669831.

32 Darren Hardy, *The Compound Effect: Jumpstart Your Income, Your Life, Your Success*, 10th anniversary edition (New York: Hachette Books, 2010), 13.

If you were given a choice between taking $3 million in cash this very instant and a single penny that doubles in value every day for 31 days, which would you choose? If you've heard this before, you know the penny gambit is the choice you should make—you know it's the course that will lead to greater wealth. Yet why is it so hard to believe choosing the penny will result in more money in the end? Because it takes so much longer to see the payoff. Let's take a closer look. Let's say you take the cold, hard cash and your friend goes the penny route. On Day Five, your friend has sixteen cents. You, however, have $3 million. On Day Ten, it's $5.12 versus your big bucks. How do you think your friend is feeling about her decision? You're spending your millions, enjoying the heck out of it, and loving your choice.

After 20 full days, with only 11 days left, Penny Lane has only $5,243. How is she feeling about herself at this point? For all her sacrifice and positive behavior, she has barely more than $5,000. You, however, have $3 million. Then the invisible magic of the Compound Effect starts to become visible. The same small mathematical growth improvement each day makes the compounded penny worth $10,737,418.24 on Day Thirty-one, more than three times your $3 million.

In this example, we see why consistency over time is so important. On Day Twenty-nine, you've got your $3 million; Penny Lane has around $2.7 million. It isn't until Day Thirty of this 31-day race that she pulls ahead, with $5.3 million. And it isn't until the very last day of this monthlong ultramarathon that your friend blows you out of the water. She ends up with $10,737,418.24 compared to your $3 million.[33]

33 Ibid., 6–7.

The same compounding principle applies to our lives. Small, consistent actions might not show big results right away, but over time, they add up to something huge. So while it might be tempting to go for the quick payoff, this simple penny example shows that sticking with steady growth and persistence often leads to much greater rewards in the end.

In *Atomic Habits*, James Clear writes, "Habits are the compound interest of self-improvement. The same way that money multiplies through compound interest, the effects of your habits multiply as you repeat them. They seem to make little difference on any given day and yet the impact they deliver over the months and years can be enormous."[34]

Over the years, I've developed these routines that keep me steady. For starters, I've always made time to exercise. While I don't always manage to work out as much as I'd like, if I can get in a session once or twice a week, it helps. Exercise has a way of clearing my mind and keeping me energized. It's one of those nonnegotiables I've held on to with rare exceptions.

Another essential piece for me is finding quiet time each morning. I'm up early, around five fifteen, and I carve out thirty to forty-five minutes just for myself. That time is precious. It's a time to read, reflect, and just be still. Starting my day like this gives me a boost that carries me through whatever's coming.

At the end of the day, I try to unwind in a similar way, sitting down with my wife to watch a show or simply be together. When I can do that, sit there holding her hand and let go of business issues or personal worries, it grounds me. Those bookends—starting the day with some quiet and ending it with stillness—keep me steady. But

---

34 Clear, *Atomic Habits*, 16.

if those routines get disrupted for a couple of weeks, I feel it. I wear down faster without them.

As Tony Robbins says in *The Compound Effect*, "Little, everyday decisions will either take you to the life you desire or to disaster by default. In fact, it's the littlest decisions that shape our lives. From what to eat and where to work, to the people you spend your time with, to how you spend your day, every choice shapes how you live today, but more importantly, how you live the rest of your life."[35]

CONFRONT YOUR BAD HABITS

Everyone has pros and cons that are often largely shaped by their personality. For example, one of my positive attributes is that I'm consistent. I aim to be balanced and not ruled by emotions. Even as a coach, I wasn't the type to get overly emotional, and that's intentional. I value consistency. I don't like to be up and down, and I try to stay even-keeled inside and out. This helps people to know what to expect, and being consistent with our emotions makes us more approachable.

The downside of this consistency is that I have an addictive personality and sometimes don't know when to take my foot off the gas. In my younger years, I went from being a sprinter in high school to a distance runner later on, and that's when I realized just how easily I could fall into this workaholic trap. I started running twenty miles a week, thinking that was good enough. But soon, I wanted to get better, so I upped it to forty miles, adding speed work and intervals.

The problem was that I didn't know when to quit. I'd push through pain, injuries, and fatigue, ending up with issues such as plantar fasciitis

---

35 Hardy, *The Compound Effect*, xxi.

that took months to heal because I couldn't bear to take a break. I'd get addicted to the grind, the thrill of pushing my limits, and that's something that's carried over into other areas of my life.

Coaching basketball gave me an adrenaline rush, and even now, I am hooked on the adrenaline of getting big things moving at work. I thrive on setting goals, rallying the team, and driving projects forward. There's an excitement in it that I get pulled into, and I could stay at it for hours. But that kind of intensity has its downside too. When I'm tired, it's harder to focus, and I'll sometimes get distracted by easier, less important tasks rather than diving into the heavy lifting. I know that about myself now, and I try to keep an eye on it, especially when I'm feeling drained.

Another bad habit I see many leaders fall into is fear. Fear is a powerful force that holds us back, especially when it comes to asking for help or being transparent about our vulnerabilities. This is particularly true for young leaders.

There's this idea that if we admit we don't know something or ask for help, we're somehow admitting weakness. Culturally, especially for men, there's an expectation to have all the answers. We don't ask for directions or help unless we absolutely have to. But for me, I found it best to lay down my pride when seeking the help I needed.

Starting out, I probably knew about 10 percent of what I needed to know to run a business. So I had no shame in having honest conversations with other business leaders and asking them questions they might have thought I should know. As I discovered, admitting what you don't know is one of the fastest ways to get the answers you need.

Another bad habit most leaders need to confront is overthinking their situation. Some people just won't take risks, and once they've experienced failure, that reluctance only grows. But failure itself teaches resilience. As I've discovered many times, failure is one of life's best teachers. People tend to get caught up in the fear of repeating their mistakes, but that fear can paralyze them. The key is to take those lessons and move forward with them.

Eldredge adds that "Life is not a problem to be solved; it is an adventure to be lived. That's the nature of it and has been since the beginning when God set the dangerous stage for this high-stakes drama and called the whole wild enterprise *good*. He rigged the world in such a way that it only works when we embrace risk as the theme of our lives, which is to say, only when we live by faith."[36]

Eldredge also writes, "Most of us do everything we can to reduce the element of risk in our lives. We wear our seat belts, watch our cholesterol, and practice birth control."[37] However, as I've observed, people who are overly structured generally don't go by faith. They go by lists.

CHALLENGING PERSONALITY TRAITS

Part of remaining true to ourselves is working through any self-limiting personality traits and refusing to become someone we're not.

By nature, I'm not a charismatic salesperson. I am not the leader who will walk into a room and always crack jokes or be the life of the party. But as the founder of a company, I inevitably found myself in situations where I'd be pulled into meetings with potential or existing customers. Despite receiving some criticism for my "dry personality," I've realized that to remain true to myself, I can't become somebody I'm not.

---

36 Eldredge, *Wild at Heart*, 183.

37 Ibid., 29.

I am who I am and cannot try to be anyone else. I'm not going to force charisma because, frankly, that's not me. Instead, I've decided that my best approach is to go into these meetings as my true self. So, in sales settings where others might dive straight into pitches or strategy, I ask simpler questions like, "How's your family?" or "What do you like to do for fun?" or "What can Master Wall do better?" You may not know what the potential or current customer needs unless you listen.

As it's turned out, those genuine conversations have often done more than any sales pitch ever could. Sometimes, just being quiet and listening turns out to be the best approach. I remind our team of that, too, that sometimes the best thing they can do for a customer is just to listen. Never underestimate the value of being likable. It can take you places you never dreamed of.

Over time, I've realized that the very area I once perceived as a negative actually helps me be a good long-term leader. I've discovered that having natural charisma carries its own set of challenges. Case in point, in *Good to Great*, Jim Collins writes, "It is worthwhile to consider the idea that charisma can be as much a liability as an asset. Your strength of personality can sow the seeds of problems, when people filter the brutal facts from you. You can overcome the liabilities of having charisma, but it does require conscious attention."[38]

So, in some ways, my lack of charisma has turned out to be a great positive. The same principle might hold true with you. Maybe you wish you had a different personality, but remember that God wired you just the way you need to be.

---

38 Collins, *Good to Great*, 73.

WHY THIS IS CHALLENGING FOR YOUNGER LEADERS

While remaining true to yourself is a challenge at any age, it's especially difficult when you're just starting out and discovering who your true self is.

Being a young leader often involves wanting to fit in and meet others' expectations. It's tempting to mold yourself into what you think a leader should be, but I always encourage emerging leaders to be genuine and embrace who they truly are. Letting go of the pressure to conform allows you to lead with authenticity.

This lesson is reinforced every month at my CEO roundtable group. This event is hosted by Georgia Tech University, and it's a place for leaders to discuss and share ideas with one another. Out of the seven-member group I am in, six are entrepreneurs. Most are over fifty, some in their sixties, and none of them are putting on a facade. They're down-to-earth, straightforward, and comfortable in their own skin. As entrepreneurs, we are free to be ourselves because we're not pressured to perform for others or compete with someone else's image of a leader.

Running your own business gives you a sense of ownership and comfort that fosters genuine leadership. I imagine that, in larger organizations, this struggle is more intense. Presidents or vice presidents in big companies often feel the need to project an image of strength or charisma, which can be stifling. But for those of us who built our businesses, we have the liberty to be ourselves, and that's a big part of what keeps us grounded.

When I was a young leader, I definitely felt insecure at times, especially when dealing with big clients. In the early days, we aimed to work with companies much larger than ours—organizations with massive sales numbers and resources far beyond our own. During those first five or ten years, I felt immense pressure to project confidence. I wanted them to see us as capable and reliable, which often meant putting on a front that I had everything under control, even when I didn't entirely feel that way. I usually felt we had to give the impression we were bigger than we were, and this was not necessary or transparent. Over the years we have produced products for companies much larger than we are through toll manufacturing.

Throughout the years, I began to feel more at ease with who I was and who our company was becoming. That confidence took time to grow, but eventually, I stopped feeling the need to overcompensate or constantly prove myself. I realized that being true to myself made me a better leader.

I see similar struggles in younger leaders today. There's often a noticeable difference between a leader who is secure and comfortable in their role and someone who is trying to project the image of the leader they think they should be. But this isn't just a problem for young leaders; this applies to leaders of any age and in any role.

I've seen leaders who have been in their organizations for forty years get very nervous when they stand up to give a presentation. Then, I've seen others with far less experience stand up and present with a sense of calm confidence. The difference wasn't knowledge or experience—it was self-assurance that comes from being comfortable with who you are.

In the end, leadership is about being genuine and embracing who you are. When you let go of the pressure to fit a mold, you can lead with authenticity and confidence. That's the kind of leadership that inspires others and fosters real connections.

BE AUTHENTIC AND KEEP VALUING OTHERS

People know when you are remaining true to yourself and when you're putting on a front. As a leader, sometimes it's tough to navigate the line between authenticity and transparency. In today's culture, especially with younger generations, authenticity is seen as a high virtue—they look to their leaders to be real and relatable. But sometimes, that can lean into a kind of "tell-all" expectation, where authenticity means sharing every last detail about yourself, including your flaws.

I believe there's a balance to strike here. Authenticity is crucial, but there's also a place for discretion. Being genuine doesn't mean laying everything bare. There are parts of ourselves that don't always need to be shared openly, especially in a professional setting.

For me, I think transparency is often more important than full-blown authenticity. I try to be open, but with discernment, knowing where to draw the line. When we're too open with others and share every dark secret from our past, this can create unnecessary tension. As one leader told me, "Don't reveal so much about your past that you scare people away and make them want to hide their silverware if they invite you into their home."

Sometimes, authenticity means being there for others and offering support through our own experiences. I think of different friends I've helped over the years who have shared some of their toughest situations with me. This is a sign of great trust, and when it comes to my own team, I treat them all with respect and openness.

Part of being authentic with others is having genuine empathy for others—regardless of their situation. In *Dignity: Seeking Respect in Back Row America*, Chris Arnade shares how his life was going well.

Despite his successes—a PhD in theoretical physics, a lucrative job as a Wall Street bond trader, a home in upscale Brooklyn, and private schooling for his kids—he saw himself as thoughtful and conscious of his privilege. He read widely, supported progressive policies, and donated to causes that addressed social inequities.

Though Arnade acknowledged his self-interest, he rationalized it by viewing himself as less selfish than others in his circles. He felt set apart from his peers because he hadn't come from wealth or attended elite prep schools, instead growing up with a professor father and a librarian mother, and attending public schools before state college. However, as he continues:

> I began to realize I hadn't ended up much different at all. I had done pretty much what successful Americans do, regardless of their politics. I had removed myself from the realities of the majority of Americans. I was a member of an exclusive club, one requiring an elite education to enter. I was sitting in my expensive home, in my exclusive neighborhood, forming opinions and casting judgments about what was best for others largely just from what I read.[39]

This set him on an adventure of a lifetime that took him to meet drug addicts, the homeless, and people who have been marginalized in so many ways. He didn't just talk to people. He spent time with them and listened to them deeply. He traveled the country in his van, capturing their stories and struggles in photos and words. The stories

---

39 Chris Arnade, *Dignity: Seeking Respect in Back Row America* (New York: Sentinel, 2019), 3.

of many of the people in his book broke my heart. I would literally catch myself tearing up as I read.

This book opened my eyes to the reality that many in our country live lives we barely understand, and it's taught me the importance of showing empathy, even to those whose struggles we might not fully grasp. When we're being open and honest, empathy should always be part of the equation. This book also reinforced my thoughts on knowing I must spend time with my people and always listen deeply.

Unfortunately, many men are taught not to show too much empathy, seeing it as a sign of weakness. But I believe that showing empathy is essential, especially when you're being transparent with others. It shows you care. You're not just unloading *your* truth but also connecting with *theirs*.

STAND BY YOUR CONVICTIONS

Remaining true to yourself means standing by your convictions, even when others don't fully understand or support them. For me, this principle has been a guidepost throughout my journey, especially in making tough decisions that weren't widely embraced. One example that comes to mind is my commitment to expanding our company's offerings beyond our traditional focus on coatings to include a line of paint—a decision that has faced plenty of pushback.

For years, I believed that broadening our product range could better position us for future economic challenges. This wasn't just an abstract idea; it came from a real, lived experience. During the Great Recession, construction projects everywhere stalled, and nearly every part of the industry took a hard hit as homeowners and businesses alike cut back on major spending. Yet, interestingly, the paint industry managed to hold steady and even grow.

People who couldn't afford renovations still wanted a change, so they opted for fresh paint to refresh their spaces. That insight stayed with me, planting a seed for the future. Paint was more than just a product; it was a practical, affordable solution that allowed people to transform their spaces during tough times. I saw how the steady demand for paint could be an anchor; a source of resilience for our company.

Since then, I've held fast to the idea that creating a versatile paint line could be a crucial part of our future. I want us to be prepared for the next economic downturn, whenever it might come, with a product that would be stable and reliable even when the rest of the market shifted. However, this idea has met with resistance within the team.

Expanding into paint isn't something our company is accustomed to; it would be a departure from our usual offerings and would come with learning curves, increased costs, and extra work. For me, though, this decision represents more than a business strategy. It's about building a sustainable future. Knowing that we could have something solid to rely on in difficult times has motivated me to stick with this vision, even if others don't yet see the full picture. I have been told repeatedly we could not compete with the big paint companies—Sherwin-Williams, Benjamin Moore, etc. Yet when you look, you discover small paint companies all over the country have a niche in their region.

Another instance where I faced a similar challenge of remaining true to my values was during the early days of our company's development. At the time, I had recently left my previous job, where I'd worked as a production manager and had gained deep insights into the industry. This experience gave me access to insider knowledge, formulas, and shortcuts that could have easily given us a head start in our new venture.

At one point, I even stumbled upon an old formula from my former employer, Dryvit. The temptation to keep it was real, especially knowing it could save us valuable time and money. It was the kind of shortcut that might have shaved years off our development timeline, an appealing thought given our tight resources back then.

But as tempting as it was, I knew that using this shortcut would compromise the foundation of integrity I wanted for our company. If we were going to build something lasting and meaningful, it had to be with our own knowledge, our own work, and on our own terms. The choice wasn't easy; I knew that letting go of the shortcut meant committing to a longer, costlier path. However, I decided to push forward without it, developing our products from scratch and relying on our own team's knowledge and abilities. It was a challenging decision, and it came with financial strains and time setbacks, but it allowed us to create something genuinely ours.

Creating our own product wasn't smooth or straightforward. We faced numerous obstacles along the way—financial limitations, production delays, and countless refinements. There were times when the setbacks felt overwhelming, and I questioned if the decision was worth it. But building it ourselves taught us invaluable lessons that no shortcut could have. It gave us an intricate understanding of our product, of every step in its process, and of the market it was meant to serve. Working from the ground up allowed us to become experts in our field in a way that borrowing or copying never would have. And it reinforced our commitment to doing things the right way, not just the easy way.

In many ways, losing my previous job had been a wake-up call—a reminder that I wanted to create a company founded on integrity, where every choice was something I could stand behind with pride. Had we taken the shortcut, I might always have felt a shadow of doubt over our achievements, wondering if they were truly ours or merely borrowed. By choosing the tougher path, we built something authentic, something that was genuinely a reflection of our values and hard work. The journey solidified my dedication to building our business with integrity, and it shaped the way we continue to approach challenges today.

Looking back, I'm grateful for these choices, even though they weren't the easiest. The products we ended up with are more than functional—they're symbols of our commitment to quality, originality, and the principle of creating something truly our own. I've learned that staying true to your values, even when it's difficult or when others don't immediately see the full picture, is always worth it. (I have to say a special thank you to our R&D person, Glen Smith, who has served in that role for over twenty-five years. He deserves a special thank-you for being totally sold on my vision of creating our products.)

This commitment to integrity has become the backbone of our company's identity, shaping who we are and what we stand for. It's a guiding principle that will continue to steer us forward, no matter what challenges or opportunities lie ahead. And it reminds me every day that building something meaningful requires patience, persistence, and a commitment to doing what's right, even when the path isn't easy.

ALWAYS GIVE GOD THE GLORY

The key to remaining true to who you are is to remember what you're worth. If you believe as I do that humans are created in the image of God, this changes everything. As a child of God, you're someone who was made with intention. And if you don't like who you are, maybe it's because you haven't fully accepted what He's created.

The great King David said in Psalm 139:14 (NKJV), "I will praise You, for I am fearfully *and* wonderfully made." When we embrace who we are—our strengths, weaknesses, and values—we live out our true identity rather than conforming to societal expectations or pretending to be someone else. We honor our Creator, who designed us with intentionality. In this way, our authentic lives become a testament to God's craftsmanship, demonstrating that we trust His plan for us and are committed to using our unique qualities to serve Him and others.

We all have flaws, we all sin, and we all make mistakes. But God understands us completely, and the ultimate way I remain true to who I've committed to be is to remain true to giving God glory in all areas of my life. When I haven't, I've lived to regret it.

For example, when I was in my early twenties, I got into running seriously. At first, I just dabbled, running a few races here and there, but every couple of years, I found myself taking it up a notch. I started with 5Ks and then began showing up at these all-comers track meets in Atlanta. They were held at some of the more elite private schools in the area, where anyone could come out and race a variety of events.

Those meets really lit a fire in me. By the time I was twenty-four, I had moved up to running 10Ks—the 6.2-mile races—and was chasing some serious goals. I was focused on breaking six-minute miles at first, and once I achieved that, I aimed for even faster paces, trying to get below five and a half minutes per mile.

Before I hung up my racing shoes, I was hitting sub-thirty-five-minute 10Ks. In local races, I'd place pretty high in my age group. It was a great feeling, knowing I was competing well and getting faster. Running became a big part of my life, and I was fully committed. I leaned down to under 150 pounds, the lightest I'd been since high school, and was in top form. In fact, I remember this one time when I applied for life insurance for my family.

They sent an in-house nurse to give me a physical, and when she checked my pulse, she looked concerned. My heart rate was just over thirty beats per minute, and she thought something was seriously wrong. She was sure I was in trouble because a "normal" resting pulse is around sixty. I tried explaining that distance runners often have lower heart rates because our bodies adapt to the training, but they still rejected me for coverage. That's how committed I was; I was in such peak condition that my pulse rate disqualified me from life insurance!

At one point, I actually believed I might be able to compete at a high level in distance running. That's when I made a commitment to God. I vowed to him that if I ever won a race, when I stepped forward to receive my medal, I would say, "To God be the glory." Well, one day, I did win a small race of around 125 people. When I went up to get my medal, I remembered my promise, but I didn't say it. It wasn't like anyone handed me the mic, but still, I didn't speak up.

Not long after that, my running career took a downturn. Injury after injury, I had to scale back and eventually stop racing. While I never blamed my injuries on not saying those words, it was a powerful lesson in integrity and keeping promises to myself and to God. When

I was doing a sales presentation to our team, my son, Steven, asked me to elaborate on this. It made a big impact on him when I spoke of it years ago. The moment I stopped being true to who God created me to be was when my body started to break down.

That experience taught me a valuable lesson. For the rest of my life, I would do everything I could not to make a name for myself but to give glory to God. As systematic theologian Wayne Grudem writes, "Our purpose must be to fulfill the reason that God created us: to glorify him."[40] Because God is the highest good, when we try to live a life that glorifies and exults self, we ultimately end up unsatisfied. But when we do everything we can to glorify Him, we enjoy life to the fullest.

A great example of this is my friend Dr. Samuel Thomas of Hopegivers International. Sam is a prominent humanitarian and spearheads the vision of "One Million Arrows" for God, aiming to rescue one million needy children from brothels, slums, and the streets of India by 2030, and to train them as global orphan leaders. Known for his dynamic leadership and strong communication skills, Sam inspires his team in India and the US to work tirelessly in advancing the Gospel and supporting children who are at risk.

Sam has had anything but an easy road. He has been imprisoned and had his life threatened many times while serving in India, spreading the Gospel and opening orphanages and Christian schools. Still, despite these difficulties, I have heard him speak multiple times, and every time he does, he says these five words, "To God be the glory!"

Sam is a living example of the fact that when you know who you are and who you want to be, you can be true to yourself regardless of the obstacles that stand in your path.

---

40 Wayne Grudem, *Systematic Theology: An Introduction to Biblical Doctrine* (Grand Rapids: Zondervan, 1994), 441.

CHAPTER 7

Build a Winning Team

LEADERS WHO DON'T LISTEN WILL EVENTUALLY BE SURROUNDED BY PEOPLE WHO HAVE NOTHING TO SAY.

—ANDY STANLEY

When you look at some of the biggest success stories in history, the constant theme is of a united team.

This is because great accomplishments are never the work of just one person. They're the result of people coming together and sharing their skills, ideas, and passions to chase a shared goal. Building a winning team isn't just about gathering talented individuals. It's about creating a collaborative spirit where the group becomes stronger than any one person could be on their own.

Think about how a concert band works. Each musician brings their own unique style and expertise, but it's the way they interact—the unspoken cues, the improvisation, and the mutual respect—that turns individual notes into unforgettable music. Similarly, in any team setting, the real magic happens when members blend their strengths and have each other's backs.

This kind of teamwork can spark innovation, solve problems more effectively, and push performance to heights that solo efforts just can't reach. As John Maxwell writes in *The 17 Indisputable Laws of Teamwork*:

> Nobody is a whole team ... We need each other. You need someone and someone needs you. Isolated islands we're not. To make this thing called life work, we gotta lean and support. And relate and respond. And give and take. And confess and forgive. And reach out and embrace and rely ... Since none of us is a whole, independent, self-sufficient, super-capable, all-powerful hotshot, let's quit acting like we are. Life's lonely enough without our playing that silly role. The game is over. Let's link up.[41]

Leaders who foster collaboration, acknowledge individual contributions, and offer constructive feedback can significantly boost their team's potential. They set the tone for accountability, continuous learning, and a shared commitment to doing something great.

DEVELOP THE MINDSET OF A COACH

One of my top five life experiences has been coaching high school boys' basketball. I love everything about the process of developing players and challenging them to be the best versions of themselves that they can be. But coaching isn't just about the thirty-two minutes

41 John C. Maxwell, *The 17 Indisputable Laws of Teamwork: Embrace Them and Empower Your Team* (Nashville: Thomas Nelson, 2001).

of whistle-to-whistle action. It's also about tough love, especially with young athletes. In basketball, perhaps more than in other settings, you develop a close bond with your players. You're deeply invested in their growth, both on and off the court.

Basketball seasons are long and stretch almost year-round. You've got summertime practices, then the season kicks off in late October, and if you're fortunate enough to make it to the playoffs, you're still playing into March. You spend so much time with these players every day—two hours of practice, traveling to games, and then the games themselves, which often last two or more hours.

Drawing up the next play with the team.

Over time, you really get to know each other, and they see everything about you, no filter. Teenagers are perceptive, and they can see right through you if you're not genuine. So, transparency and fairness are essential to earning their respect.

Watching a player improve over the course of a season, seeing them work hard, buy into the process, and start to believe in themselves—that's the ultimate reward. As John Maxwell writes, "Good things happen to a team when a player takes the place where he adds the most value. Great things happen when all the players on the team take the role that maximizes their strengths—their talent, skill, and experience."[42]

In the moment my players broke through and reached a new level, knowing I'd had a hand in that progress was incredibly fulfilling. And when a team comes together and clicks, it's magic. There were a couple of seasons where I had enough good players to employ the two-platoon system, which meant I could send in five fresh players, pull them out after a few minutes, and send in another five.

Those were some of the best years. I had a roster full of athletic, talented players who understood the game. I could just let them loose on the court, and they'd deliver. Those seasons were less about constant coaching and more about enjoying the flow of the game. Then, of course, there were seasons when I wished for more timeouts because I needed to constantly pull the guys aside, talk through plays, and keep them on track. With those teams, it was a lot more hands-on, coaching them on the details, pulling out the clipboard, drawing up plays, and hoping that enough preparation had sunk in.

Good teams have chemistry. Author Don Yaeger put it this way. He writes that great teams have:

Targeting Purpose—The team is connected to a greater purpose. Members understand whom they are serving and why that matters.

Effective Management—The team is able to think creatively and act dynamically in order to stay fresh, effective, and relevant.

Activating Efficiency—Each member of the team brings a unique set of talents, experiences, perspectives, work ethic, personality traits,

42 Ibid.

and know-how that melds with and complements those of the other team members.

Mutual Direction—There is a strong sense of understanding, appreciation, shared responsibility, and trust that unites and motivates the team to work together.[43]

In a good team, players get along, they're talented, and, most importantly, they *want* to be a team. When that desire to work together is there, you can feel it as the season progresses. Sure, the season might start a bit rough, but over time, you can see the rhythm take shape as they support each other on and off the court.

On the flip side, if there's a lot of dissent or if the players don't even like each other, it's hard to form a championship team. You might win a few games on talent alone, but it's nearly impossible to go the distance without unity. It's a lot like a workplace team—whether it's accounting or production, if they don't get along, if there's constant friction, productivity and efficiency are going to suffer.

At the end of the day, coaching has been one of the greatest joys of my life. It was challenging, rewarding, and humbling all at once. I learned so much about leadership and teamwork from those players, and they shaped me as much as I shaped them.

PREPARE AND PLAY HARD

When it comes to coaching, preparation is absolutely critical. Game-day adjustments are important, but most of the heavy lifting happens beforehand.

Years ago, I'd have my team spend hours watching film, studying each team we were going to face. Now, with digital access, it's even

---

43 Don Yaeger, *Great Teams: 16 Things High-Performing Organizations Do Differently* (Nashville: W Publishing Group, 2016), xvii.

easier, but the goal is the same: understanding the opponent's strengths, weaknesses, and style of play, and identifying the players who excel at rebounding, shooting, or running particular plays. Preparation is all about knowing what we're up against and figuring out how to match it with the strengths of our own team.

I was what some might call a "practice coach." For me, everything came down to the way we ran our sessions. Every drill had a purpose, and every minute was timed. We set the clock for five or ten minutes per drill, and we'd run it hard, focusing the whole time. If something wasn't going well, we'd stop, go over what needed to improve, then set the clock and start again. This high-paced approach kept players plugged in and engaged.

Because teenagers often lose focus quickly, it's important to keep them moving, active, and focused. I often repeated to them that phrase I used earlier in this book: "What you focus on prospers." One of the benefits of running a fast-paced practice is that we rarely needed separate conditioning sessions.

I always coached my players to work hard. Admittedly, sometimes this model didn't always go over well in a private Christian school setting. Because my teams were intense, sometimes I encountered parents from other teams who thought that playing aggressively didn't align with Christian values. Some even suggested that we shouldn't push the boys so hard, that it wasn't Christian to play so tough and aggressively. But I saw it differently. I wanted to teach these young men resilience, strength, and the value of hard work. I wanted to show them what proper preparation and hard work could accomplish. And I wanted to help build their character by pushing them outside their comfort zones, whether in practice or playing the game.

The same principles apply to forming a great business team. Great teams in any organization are formed by being challenged and coached to achieve a compelling vision. In the words of Michael Jordan, "Talent wins games, but teamwork and intelligence win championships."[44]

COACH WITH GRACE

Because every team member is different, each requires a unique coaching approach. For example, I coached my star players differently than I coached someone who was newer to the game and hadn't developed his skills. If a player struggled with shooting, for instance, I'd make sure they got extra time working with a coach whose specialty was shooting. After practice, they'd spend time shooting jumpers, getting that individual attention. It was less about being hard on them and more about guiding them, coaching them, and investing the time they needed to grow.

Over time, I've come to see coaching as a form of discipleship that helps players think and live more like Christ. It's not just about disciplining players to improve—it's about mentoring them and helping them find their way. Looking back, I wish I'd had a similar approach when I was raising my own kids. I was often quick to discipline rather than disciple.

Now, I try to bring grace into everything I do, whether it's basketball, work, or life. As leadership author Andy Stanley writes, "Grace is understood best within the context of relationship."[45] Grace allows space for growth, for learning, and for patience.

When you approach coaching—or life—from a place of grace, it becomes about more than winning games. It becomes about shaping character, building resilience, and nurturing young people to be their

44 Grant Freeland, "Talent Wins Games, Teamwork Wins Championships," *Forbes*, June 1, 2018, https://www.forbes.com/sites/grantfreeland/2018/06/01/talent-wins-games-teamwork-wins-championships/.

45 Andy Stanley, *The Grace of God* (Nashville: Thomas Nelson, 2010), 8.

best selves. Christian musician Matthew West wrote a song, "Grace Wins," which became one of my key coaching mottos as I worked with kids and employees of differing abilities. Personally, I respond much better to grace than being punished. This probably comes from having a father for whom grace wasn't an option.

Leading at different levels also means knowing when someone is ready for a new responsibility and being cautious not to push them too soon. With basketball, parents often focus only on *their* child. They want them to play more, even if the timing or situation isn't right. But what they don't see is how much of a negative impact this can have on the kids.

So over lunch or after practice, I would explain to parents that I wanted their child to play just as much as they did, but putting them in a game at the wrong time could damage their confidence and cause them to lose their love for the sport altogether. In work, it's similar—promoting someone too early or putting them in a challenging situation before they're ready can set them up for failure. It's our job as leaders to understand our people well enough to gauge when they're ready for the next step, because we want them to be successful.

We have grace when they mess up and the resolve to not promote them before their abilities are where they need to be. This is why taking time to develop people, to understand their strengths, and to let them grow naturally into roles is so important. It's about setting people up for success, not just to meet their personal goals but for the greater good of the team and the organization. If you handle this right, your team members will thrive.

CARE ABOUT THOSE YOU LEAD

Whether you're coaching a basketball team or leading an organization, the basic tenets of leadership remain the same. As leadership author Tod Bolsinger writes, leadership is "energizing a community of people toward their own transformation in order to accomplish a shared mission in the face of a changing world."[46]

In both roles, you've got to genuinely care about the people you're guiding. You have to love them and then lead them. Whether it's athletes on the court or employees in a business, people pick up quickly on it if you're only halfway invested.

Building confidence is essential in both roles, and that confidence has to come from knowing your goals and being prepared. Whether you're laying out a game plan or a company vision, you have to know the direction you're headed, be transparent about it, and then lead your team toward those shared objectives. They have to buy in to your plans and goals.

They need to know you are genuine, that they can trust you, and that you're willing to invest in them. With both coaching and business leadership, you're not just driving results; you're helping shape individuals, encouraging them to grow and reach their potential. In business, you're working more on strategic goals that might involve quarterly results, metrics, or projects, while in coaching, it's often about honing skills for specific performance outcomes, such as a win on game day. But in either case, people follow leaders they trust and respect, so taking the time to know each team member, learning their strengths and weaknesses, and supporting their growth is key.

---

46 Tod Bolsinger, *Canoeing the Mountains: Christian Leadership in Uncharted Territory* (Downers Grove: InterVarsity Press, 2018), 42.

Thankfully, my leadership and coaching abilities today are a far cry from what they used to be. When I was working as a leader at Dryvit in my mid-thirties, my approach was tougher than it is today. Back then, the leadership style was pretty intense, and confrontations weren't uncommon.

Today, whether in sports or in business, people want to be led differently. They resist authoritarian styles of leadership and want to work for people whom they think have their best interests at heart. In the past, I allowed situations to escalate and the temperature in the room to rise. Now, I try to handle conflict by remaining calm and composed.

When those on your team recognize you care about them, they're much more willing to forgive your mistakes and give you the benefit of the doubt. This is something you can practice at any position within an organization. In any role, whether leading those below, beside, or above you, it all starts with helping others move forward. I always say that the best way to climb the corporate ladder is to push the person ahead of you up the rungs.

Be encouraging of those around you, create an environment of shared success, be transparent, and genuinely want the best for those you lead. When you take these steps, you become the leader others want to follow.

DO THE LITTLE THINGS WELL

In leadership, the little things are often the most impactful, and they go beyond the big-picture strategy or in-game adjustments. A core concept I've tried to embrace and pass along is servant leadership. As Robert Greenleaf writes, servant leadership "begins with the natural feeling that one wants to serve, to serve first. Then conscious choice brings one to aspire to lead. That person is sharply different from one who is leader first, perhaps because of the need to assuage an unusual power drive or to acquire material possessions."[47]

Servant leadership is not a new concept, but it's one that changes people's outlook on management and executive roles. A servant leader aims to empower, nurture, and guide others, fostering a culture of trust, collaboration, and shared growth. This style contrasts with traditional top-down leadership by valuing humility, empathy, and active listening. Ultimately, servant leadership seeks to inspire and elevate others, creating a ripple effect of positive change and strong, ethical organizations.

I think of a story I read about a Chick-fil-A executive who was seen picking up trash along the exit ramp near the company's home office. He cared about the impression that the road made on visitors, and instead of delegating the job, he did it himself. That's the kind of leadership that earns respect and resonates with people.

As Master Wall has grown, I have relied on our plant managers to keep me updated on the lives of employees on the floor. I want to know what's going on in their lives and the challenges they're facing. When I walk through the plant, I try to connect with those team members directly, whether it's asking about a family member's health or a personal concern they're dealing with. It's a balancing act, though, because as the organization expands, it becomes harder to know every employee personally. But I make an effort to stay informed and to show empathy whenever possible.

Creating a culture that reflects your core values goes far beyond simply establishing guidelines or policies. It requires you to embody those values in your everyday actions. As a leader, your behavior sets

---

47 Robert K. Greenleaf, *Servant Leadership: A Journey into the Nature of Legitimate Power and Greatness*, 25th anniversary edition, ed. Larry C. Spears (New York: Paulist Press, 2002), 346.

the tone for what is truly important, and your team will take their cues from what they see you do, not just what they hear you say.

BE A GOOD LISTENER

Sometimes as a leader, it's easy to get so focused on everything that's happening that you lose sight of the details. This is why it's so important to listen to those key voices around you. As a head coach, having assistant coaches on the bench taught me a lot about the importance of perspective. In the heat of the game, I could be so focused on every play, every call, that sometimes I missed the details.

My assistant coaches often made suggestions that kept me on track. One might say, "Hey, Joe was on fire in the first quarter. Why not put him back in the game?" And often, they were right because they saw something I overlooked. I was focused on defense and my assistant coach was figuring out how to score more points.

Listening to other perspectives is critical, especially when promoting people or trying to place them in the right roles. Those around you may notice strengths or issues that you've missed, so it's valuable to take their input seriously. As Simon Sinek says, "Communication is not about speaking, it's about listening."[48]

Listening is a fundamental skill that goes beyond simply hearing words. It involves actively engaging with and understanding the speaker's message, intentions, and emotions. When we listen attentively, we demonstrate respect, empathy, and a genuine interest in the other person's perspective, building trust and fostering stronger relationships.

In leadership, effective listening is essential because it allows you to understand the needs and concerns of your team, make informed decisions, and create a culture of openness and inclusivity. Ultimately,

---

48 Sinek, *Start with Why* (New York: Portfolio), 160.

listening is a key component of emotional intelligence that helps you connect more deeply with others and respond thoughtfully, rather than react impulsively.

If you're a younger leader, listening is especially important. Humility and patience are essential. It's easy to want rapid advancement, but rushing can sometimes backfire. If you're doing good work and adding value, especially in our organization, you'll likely be noticed and rewarded in time. So keep asking questions and keep listening.

CREATE A GENEROUS ENVIRONMENT

One of the best ways to create a great team atmosphere is to create a generous environment. There is something about generosity that changes a workplace environment. To this point, in *Living Life Backward*, David Gibson asks, "What if our work was never intended to make us successful but simply to make us faithful and generous?"[49]

When teammates learn how to "share the ball," it creates a ripple effect throughout the organization. There are countless little ways to be a generous leader. For example, I often have employees asking for support, whether it's sponsoring a local sports team or buying snacks for a fundraiser. I try to say yes to these requests and make sure the gesture extends to the entire team—buying enough for everyone to share. It's not about making a grand statement. It's about genuinely valuing the people you work with and showing that in small, consistent ways.

To me, if our company's culture isn't generous and supportive, it's a failure on my part as a leader. Generosity isn't just a nice-to-have. It's a core principle of running a successful business. It's about

---

49 David Gibson, *Living Life Backward: How Ecclesiastes Teaches Us to Live in Light of the End* (Wheaton: Crossway, 2017), 45.

investing in people and demonstrating that the company cares more about building a strong, respectful team than about maximizing profit. When leaders model these values authentically and consistently, it sets a tone that spreads naturally, creating a culture where generosity and support become the norm, not the exception.

Some people might say, "I'd rather have more money than a pat on the back." And this makes a degree of sense. Everyone wants to feel financially valued. However, if you want generosity to become part of your organization's core DNA, it has to be practiced consistently, even when it isn't immediately reciprocated.

True generosity often feels counterintuitive, especially when you sense that the recipient might not give anything in return. But this mindset misses the essence of genuine giving. You don't give with the expectation of receiving something in return; you give because it aligns with your values and the kind of culture you want to foster. Over time, this type of authentic generosity can inspire others, creating a ripple effect throughout the organization where giving becomes a shared, natural practice.

It's important to combine both recognition and rewards. A bonus, a gift card, or even a simple handwritten note can have a big impact. As leadership expert Andy Stanley says, "What gets celebrated gets repeated."[50] When someone goes above and beyond, make sure they feel seen and appreciated.

For instance, when I first hired our CFO, she struggled with my habit of giving unplanned bonuses for exceptional work. It wasn't in the budget, but I'd tell her, "That's OK, let's do it anyway." Over time, she saw the value in these gestures and even started budgeting

---

50 Leading Worship Well, "What Gets Celebrated Gets Repeated," accessed November 15, 2024, https://www.leadingworshipwell.com/blogposts/what-gets-celebrated-gets-repeated.

for them, recognizing how small acts of generosity reinforce a culture of care and appreciation.

As a coach, I kept hats and T-shirts on hand as rewards for outstanding effort. If I focused on defense, I might reward any player who drew an offensive foul during a game with a special T-shirt featuring Master Wall's logo. These shirts became a badge of honor, worn proudly by players, reinforcing the emphasis on strong defense. This simple practice of celebrating specific achievements helps build a team that plays with intensity and pride.

There are countless ways to be generous. For example, if a member of your team reaches out suggesting you recognize employees who come in during their vacation to handle urgent issues without expecting anything in return, take that opportunity. Their initiative and dedication deserve recognition, and you should make sure they know it's appreciated.

Generosity should be a constant, even during challenging seasons. Whether your organization is experiencing rapid growth or navigating tough economic times like the 2008 financial crisis, the foundation of your leadership approach should remain steady. During lean periods, the rewards might be smaller, but the principle stays the same: Acknowledge hard work and reward dedication.

By adjusting your approach without losing the spirit of gratitude, you can maintain morale and show your team that their efforts are valued, even when financial constraints require some adjustments. Across all seasons, whether times are good or difficult, your core values—generosity, recognition, and consistency—should stay unwavering. While unique situations may call for slight shifts in how you handle things, the commitment to these principles remains steadfast.

BUILD A CONTAGIOUS CULTURE

As Walter Isaacson notes in *The Innovators*, "One problem with successful teams, particularly intense ones, is that sometimes they break up. It takes a special type of leader—inspiring yet also nurturing, competitive yet collaborative—to hold such teams together."[51] There's also a prevalent mindset among younger generations that loyalty is a myth and that your boss doesn't have your best interests at heart.

I understand where that thinking comes from, but I believe a strong culture can make a difference. At Master Wall, we aim to demonstrate that longevity has rewards, not just financially but in terms of career growth and fulfillment. We pay well, and the longer you're with us, the better your opportunities and compensation. My hope is that our culture is strong enough to encourage people to stay, grow with us, and find satisfaction here rather than constantly seeking the next opportunity.

Does turnover happen? Of course—especially with entry-level roles on the production floor. But we try to minimize this as much as possible. We often use temp services initially, which allows us to evaluate fit before making a long-term commitment. If a new hire isn't the right fit, we can bring in someone else through the temp agency. This way, we can maintain a team of people who genuinely want to be here and are engaged with our mission.

As I look toward the future and the idea of stepping back, I think a lot about sustainability and passing on the company culture. I want our key leaders to embody the values we've built over the years. Our mission statement isn't just a document—it's the foundation of who

---

51 Walter Isaacson, *The Innovators: How a Group of Hackers, Geniuses, and Geeks Created the Digital Revolution* (New York: Simon & Schuster, 2014), 152.

we are, and I regularly emphasize it, especially with those who don't work in our main office.

For instance, in one of our sales meetings, I spent my presentation time going through the mission statement, reinforcing the culture and values with our sales team, many of whom work remotely. It's critical that our leaders and team members are united in these values because they'll be the ones carrying this forward.

Ultimately, I hope our culture is contagious. If our core principles resonate with those who've been with us long enough, they'll naturally pass it on, creating a sustainable legacy. It's not just about business continuity; it's about preserving the spirit of the company we've worked so hard to build.

BE THE LEADER OTHERS WANT TO FOLLOW

In the end, as John Maxwell says, "Everything rises and falls on leadership."[52]

If your team isn't where you want it to be, the responsibility starts with you. As Lieutenant General George Flynn wrote, "I know of no case study in history that describes an organization that has been managed out of a crisis. Every single one of them was led."[53] In the words of the great American Ford automobile executive Lee Iacocca, "The speed of the boss is the speed of the team."[54]

---

52 John C. Maxwell, *The 360 Degree Leader: Developing Your Influence from Anywhere in the Organization* (Nashville: Thomas Nelson, 2005).

53 Simon Sinek, *Leaders Eat Last: Why Some Teams Pull Together and Others Don't* (New York: Portfolio, 2014), Kindle edition, xi.

54 Bill Green, "Building a Company Culture That Is Fast and Efficient Starts with the Founder. Here's Why," *Inc.*, June 26, 2018, https://www.inc.com/bill-green/the-speed-of-boss-is-speed-of-team-heres-why-founders-need-to-set-pace.html.

Building a great team takes a lot of time and intentionality. Just talking about how things should be won't cut it if people aren't seeing that commitment consistently in action. If things aren't as you would like them to be right now, don't get frustrated and berate those around you. Don't be the coach who allows his frustration to trickle down to the players on the floor.

Instead, resolve to act with integrity, empathy, and respect; others will take notice, and gradually, the energy around you can start to shift. If you're at the top, changing culture means being intentional every day about setting the right example. If the mission statement says one thing, your actions need to say the same thing, without exception. The same message applies if you sit lower on the org chart.

When I think of leaders who have modeled this well, I think of business owner S. Truett Cathy, the founder of Chick-fil-A. Cathy built his company on unwavering Christian values, emphasizing integrity, humility, and service. One of his most notable decisions was closing Chick-fil-A on Sundays, a tradition maintained since 1946. This choice wasn't based on profit but on his belief in honoring a day of rest and giving employees time with family, even though it meant losing significant revenue. By consistently prioritizing people over profits, Cathy set a powerful example for his entire organization.

Cathy's leadership approach was rooted in servant leadership, where he led by example and consistently showed care for his employees, calling them "team members" instead of staff. He offered scholarships, training, and career development opportunities, believing in investing in his people as the key to long-term success. His consistency in applying these values created a unique company culture focused on exceptional service, hospitality, and genuine care for both customers and employees. As a result, Chick-fil-A became known for its loyal customer base, outstanding service, and a team that embodies the company's principles. In Cathy's words, "The people are more important than the food."[55]

This strong, value-driven culture also helped Chick-fil-A navigate challenges and rapid growth without compromising its core identity. Even during economic downturns, Cathy maintained his focus on quality and integrity, opting not to cut corners for short-term gains. His steadfast commitment inspired loyalty and a strong sense of purpose among employees, turning Chick-fil-A into one of the most profitable and respected fast-food chains in America.

Although I've never strived to be a leader, it seems I have constantly ended up in a position of leadership. Part of this is because I genuinely like people, and I believe that has made me likable to my peers. As I often say to my team, "Never underestimate the value of being likable. It can take you places you never dreamed you could go."

I try to be the leader others want to follow.

BE CONSISTENT, BE AUTHENTIC, AND DON'T SETTLE

In conclusion, there are three challenges I want to leave you with: Be consistent, be authentic, and don't settle. These are the pillars of everything I've done. They are simple, but they've had a profound impact on how I lead, how I build relationships, and how I've approached every challenge.

Consistency is so important, and I've tried my best to show up with the same values every day, whether I'm at work or at home. I never wanted there to be a different version of me based on the setting. Consistency builds trust because people know what to expect from

---

55 S. Truett Cathy, "S. Truett Cathy Quotes," BrainyQuote, accessed November 14, 2024, https://www.brainyquote.com/quotes/s_truett_cathy_699454.

you. They can count on your word, and they can rely on you to make decisions based on the same principles, regardless of the circumstances.

It's easy to be consistent when things are going well, but the real test is how you show up during the tough times. That's when your values matter most. I believe that if you can stay true to who you are and what you believe in, it sets the tone for the entire organization. It creates a culture of stability, reliability, and trust, which is essential for a winning team.

Authenticity is another principle I've tried to live by. In today's world, it's all too common to see people putting on a facade, trying to be what they think others want them to be. But the problem with that is it's not sustainable. Eventually, the mask slips, and the disconnect becomes clear.

True authenticity requires vulnerability. It means being open about your mistakes, your fears, and your uncertainties. It's not always easy, but it's what builds genuine connections. People can sense when you're being real, and that honesty is what creates trust. It's what makes people want to follow you, not because they have to but because they believe in you. When you lead with authenticity, you create an environment where others feel safe to be themselves as well. That's when creativity and innovation thrive, and that's when teams do their best work.

The last principle is a simple one, but it's just as crucial: *Don't settle*. It's easy to become comfortable once you've had a bit of success. There's a temptation to rest on your laurels, to look at what you've achieved and think you've done enough. But the moment you stop pushing for more, you start to stagnate. Growth comes from challenging yourself, stepping outside your comfort zone, and striving for something better.

I've always believed that life is a journey of continuous improvement. It's not about being dissatisfied with what you have; it's about recognizing that there's always room to grow, to learn, and to become better. Settling means missing out on opportunities you didn't even know were possible. It's choosing the safe route when the path less traveled could lead to something extraordinary. For me, it's been about setting high standards for myself and my team, not because we have to, but because we owe it to ourselves to see what we're truly capable of.

These three principles—be consistent, be authentic, and don't settle—are interconnected in a way that creates a strong foundation for both life and leadership. Consistency without authenticity can feel hollow, like going through the motions without any real passion behind it. Authenticity without consistency can seem unreliable, as if you're blowing in the wind without any guiding force. And if you settle, it doesn't matter how authentic or consistent you are because you're not striving to reach your full potential. Together, they form a powerful trio that has guided me through every season of my life.

So hold on to these values tightly. Let them be your compass, guiding you through the highs and the lows. Be consistent in how you show up, be true to who you are, and never settle for less than you're capable of. Keep pushing yourself, keep growing, and never stop striving to be the best version of yourself. That's how you make a difference that lasts far beyond your own time.

If you can do that, you won't just build a winning team—you'll build a life that's meaningful, fulfilling, and impactful. You'll leave behind a legacy that others can learn from and be inspired by, and that's the greatest achievement of all.

CONCLUSION

If there is one feeling I have as I bring this book to a close, it's gratitude. I am deeply grateful for the many wonderful people I've had the chance to meet and the powerful experiences I've had. Through every setback and every challenge, I've felt blessed beyond measure. I never take for granted the privilege of working alongside family and such an incredible team.

We've built something special—a place where we can provide not just jobs, but security, benefits, and a fair wage. Knowing that we're able to make a positive impact in the lives of our employees and their families is the greatest reward I could ask for. It's about more than the business itself; it's about being a ministry. It's about building a legacy of care, respect, and community. That's why every struggle and every ounce of effort was worth it. Now that I'm in my seventies, I can look back and say with certainty that this journey, with all its ups and downs, has been incredibly fulfilling.

True success, as I've discovered, isn't a solo endeavor. Everyone plays a role, and it's the people who showed up every day, who brought their best selves to work, who made sacrifices and shared in the vision that truly made this journey worthwhile. I think of individuals like Mike Irving, Dennis Deppner, Greg Wright, Ryan Whiting, Jeff

Knight, Jeff Muir, Leo Crowell, Brian Conroy, Debbie Wetherington, Deborah Culpepper, Brad Summerall, Jesse Mildton, Danny Harley, Jermario Green, Carolynn Nale, and Wendy Long—these are the folks who went above and beyond, who turned dreams into reality. I could go on naming names because so many people have contributed in ways big and small.

While many my age feel anxious about the future, I can honestly say I am more hopeful today than ever. A large reason for this is my faith. It has been the bedrock of everything I've done. It's what gave me the strength to keep going when the path was unclear, to trust that my efforts had a purpose even when I couldn't see the end.

I've always believed that my role was to trust, believe, and work as hard as I could. There's a deep joy that comes from that kind of trust—a joy that isn't dependent on circumstances but comes from knowing that whatever happens, it's part of a bigger plan. True peace, I've learned, doesn't come from a life without challenges. It comes from the assurance that there's meaning and purpose behind it all, even when we can't understand it in the moment.

In "Chapter 1: Reach Your Tipping Point," I reflected on the shock of suddenly losing my job, which felt like much more than just a career setback—it turned my whole life upside down. Faced with uncertainty, I had a choice: stay stuck in despair or turn this challenge into an opportunity.

This chapter is a reminder that life's toughest moments can actually spark the most meaningful growth and transformation. Starting Master Wall wasn't a strategic career move; it was a leap of faith driven by the need to provide for my family and hold on to the values that had guided me all my life.

That initial tipping point, as overwhelming as it was, became the foundation for what Master Wall is today. It's a reminder that a tipping point doesn't always look like an obvious opportunity. It often comes disguised as hardship, uncertainty, or even failure. But these challenging moments can be the very ones that open doors to new paths and new purposes, letting us build something beyond what we ever imagined.

In "Chapter 2: Never, Never, Never Give Up," I wrote about the power of persistence—something I learned early on. Growing up, I faced challenges on the athletic field and in life that taught me the importance of finishing what I started. Those early lessons became invaluable as I faced business setbacks that tested my determination.

This chapter emphasizes that success isn't about avoiding failure; it's about rising each time we fall. Persistence isn't a rare trait gifted to the elite few. It's a tool *everyone* can develop. By sharing my journey, I hope to show others that persistence, combined with purpose and strong values, can be a powerful force. It's not something you're born with—it's a choice you make over and over again when faced with obstacles.

"Chapter 3: Face Your Near-Death Experiences" dives into the ups and downs of entrepreneurship. Success doesn't follow a straight path. It's a series of high points that inspire us and low points that challenge us. It was in those low moments—when everything seemed to go wrong—that I learned the most about resilience and faith. This chapter emphasizes that setbacks aren't failures. They're essential lessons that prepare us for the next peak.

This chapter is a reminder that both the highs and the lows matter. The tough times force us to reflect, grow, and strengthen our commitment to the path we've chosen. True success isn't just about reaching the peak. It's about enduring the valleys that make each victory sweeter. This chapter is a message of hope—no matter how dark or difficult things may seem, there's always a way forward if we keep climbing.

In "Chapter 4: Make Decisions for the Right Reasons," I discuss building a business grounded in integrity. For me, Master Wall was never just about profit. It was about creating something that reflected my commitment to my family, my team, my community, and maybe my ministry. This chapter highlights that lasting success doesn't come from shortcuts. In a world often focused on quick gains, it's about holding true to our core values.

When faced with tough decisions, my commitment to integrity was always my guiding star. By building Master Wall on honesty, respect, and quality, I created not just a successful business but a lasting legacy. This chapter challenges readers to stay true to their values, even when the right choice is the hardest one. It's a reminder that the best businesses—and lives—are built on purpose, trust, and authenticity.

In "Chapter 5: Notice Everyone's Strengths," I share the importance of recognizing each person's unique talents. Early on, I realized that success wasn't just about my own efforts. It was about creating a team where everyone's strengths could shine. By embracing diversity within my team, I fostered loyalty, collaboration, and a shared vision.

This chapter offers a valuable lesson for leaders and anyone looking to build a supportive community. True success isn't about molding people into a specific role but about seeing their potential, even when it doesn't fit a traditional mold. I've seen firsthand that when we value diverse skills and perspectives, we create an environment where everyone can thrive. It's a call to embrace differences, seeing them not as challenges but as strengths we can tap into.

"Chapter 6: Remain True to Who You've Committed to Be" explores the journey of staying authentic under pressure. Building Master Wall wasn't just about scaling a business. It was about staying rooted in the values I was raised with. Despite external pressures, I held fast to honesty, fairness, and transparency. This chapter shows that real success comes when we stay aligned with who we truly are and what we believe.

In a world where external pressures often try to steer us off course, staying true to ourselves takes real courage. This chapter encourages readers to pursue authenticity in both their personal and professional lives, reminding us that success without staying true to who we are is empty. Real fulfillment comes from building a life that reflects our deepest values.

Finally, in "Chapter 7: Build a Winning Team," I discuss the importance of mentorship. Throughout my career, I've been committed to guiding others and investing in their growth. Real leadership is about serving others, not just pursuing personal goals. By mentoring and supporting others, I've built a legacy that goes beyond the walls of my company.

This chapter is a reminder that our legacy isn't just about what we achieve—it's about the lives we impact. By investing in people, we create a positive ripple effect that lasts far beyond our own time. It's a call for all of us to embrace leadership and mentorship, to lift others up, and to redefine success as something we share, not just something we achieve on our own.

The story of Master Wall, with all its ups and downs, reminds me that true success isn't just about what I achieve but about how I live, what I believe in, and how I handle adversity. This book, at its core, is an invitation to see life as a chance to build something meaningful, anchored in values that go beyond fleeting gains or material rewards.

Reflecting on my journey, I see that the path to success is about much more than professional achievements. It's about resilience, values, and the courage to pursue a vision rooted in integrity. For anyone facing similar challenges, I hope this book offers you encouragement and practical wisdom. Life is full of challenges, and the way forward is rarely simple, but no obstacle is too great for those grounded in their values and committed to making a difference.

As you reflect on my story, I invite you to examine the motivations behind your own journey. Success is only truly meaningful when it aligns with our deepest values. We can build something that benefits ourselves and contributes positively to others' lives.

The story of Master Wall is ultimately about creating a legacy beyond financial success. It's about building a life of meaning, rooted in timeless principles. Whether you are just beginning your journey, are in the midst of a struggle, or have reached a peak, I hope my story inspires you to live with resilience, lead with integrity, and build a life that reflects your highest values.

One of the most important lessons I've tried to pass on, especially to my kids, is that peace and happiness are often a matter of choice. I used to say, "Do you know how to be happy? Be happy." It sounds simple, almost too simple, but that mindset has carried me through more tough times than I can count.

When faced with difficulties, we all have a choice in how we respond. We can choose to dwell on the negative, or we can choose to focus on what's good and what's still possible. It's that choice, that attitude of gratitude and positivity, that's been the backbone of my life. Without it, I might have given up when things got tough.

Instead, I leaned into faith, trusted the process, and found joy in the journey. With God's grace, I will never, never, never give up and will always give Him the glory!

ACKNOWLEDGMENTS

Most of all I am deeply grateful for my family—Donnie, Steven, Natalie, Grant, and Stewart. Every member of my family helped and worked in Master Wall with me at the beginning. Natalie started a family with her husband, Brad Snow, and with five kids she had to change her priorities. My three sons have been totally committed through the years. My grandson Blake has even committed to a career with the company. As I have said in my dedication, my wife, Donnie, made this possible.

Thanks also to:

My mom and dad, Dorothy and Gerald Smithwick—so thankful for my mom's confidence and encouragement and my dad's commitment to jump in and help me.

None of this would have been possible without the many team members who have joined me over the years on this journey to start, build, and finish this dream. A special thank you to Jay Bonner, who became my first full-time employee and did everything possible to help me. He became my quality control specialist, production manager, supervisor, and colorist. In fact, he may be the most dependable man I've ever known. Unending gratitude to Mike Irving, who decided to join Master Wall over twenty-five years ago. Mike brought his ability to create and execute a plan at a time it was badly needed. Mike did more than anyone to help shape our culture and values. We wouldn't be the company we are without his investment in us. He has been loyal and committed his entire career with us. Dennis Deppner, our technical services manager, transformed our company's technical department into the best in the industry. Ted DeVit, who took us to another level with his abilities to get us through early testing hurdles. Our salesmen mean it when they label him an all-star. He has been a huge key to our success. To Jeff Muir, Leo Crowell, DJ Mein, Ryan Whiting, Mateo Navarro, Greg Wright, Brian Conroy, Dave and Phil Neff, CJ Maywell, Mark Martin, Regi Mendoza, Jeff Knight, Glen Smith, Brad Summerall, Sharon Brown, Nelson Garcia, Jermario Green, Andre Hickson, Danny Harley, Jesse Mildton, Sonrayshaun Howard, Stephen Miller, Carolynn Nale, Amanda Collier, Wendy Long, Debbie Wetherington, Deborah Culpepper, Jacob Purcell, and Susan Ellis—thank you for your work on every detail to make Master Wall a success.

Steve Davis and Billy Joe Donaldson—for their investment of their commitment and resources to start Master Wall.

Don Wilhite—Thank you for teaching me to never, never, never give up.

Jay Dye—Thank you for demonstrating grace to me.

Cecil Cheves, Jerry Watts, Rusty Hinds, Jim Clark, and all the attorneys at Page, Scrantom, Sprouse, Tucker & Ford for their valuable council over the years.

Bob Gilson—Thank you for being the best landlord a business could ask for. Master Wall has leased your buildings for nearly thirty years. You have been fair, honest, helpful, and flexible.

All those former basketball players I coached. You have no idea what it does to my spirit when I see you somewhere and you call me *Coach*.

All the assistant coaches that helped me over the years and for the advice that made me look good—Kevin Williams, Scott Jones, Grant Smithwick, Rodney Morris, and Paul Hovey.

All those people who helped run the men's basketball program—Mike Getkin, John Tucker, and Brian Osborne. Thank you, Mike Carr, Renny Price, Wayne Smith, Jonathan Brasher, Brad Summerall, Jason Ketchum, Linda Carr, Susan Gray, Diane Johnson, Stuart Mills, Mark Walker, and all those I failed to mention here, but who were so valuable. And as with anything I've done, my wife, Donnie, helped by washing dozens and dozens of loads of towels for the team.

Stuart Mills-Wells—who made himself part of our teams from the time he was five or six years old until he was a player doing anything he could to be involved with our teams. I am proud now to see him as an assistant coach for Columbus State University. His love for the game seems to never change.

All those who invested in this book at Advantage—Nate Best, Elizabeth Brueggemann, Annie LaGreca, and Megan Elger, with special thanks to Ezra Byer for helping shape *Believer, Bulldog, Coach* into its best form.

APPENDIX

Weekly Positive Emails

JANUARY 2021

Team,

I am a day or two late in getting a positive message to you. We are really fortunate as a business to have a lot going on. Lots of good stuff too. This leads me right into the positive message from the book by Dan Green, *Finish Strong* with the subtitle—More than a statement … it's an attitude:

"Success seems to be connected with action. Successful people keep moving. They make mistakes, but they don't quit."—Conrad Hilton

I love "don't quit." As I have said numerous times, "Never, never, never give up."

FEBRUARY 2021

Team,

There are many reasons for sending out the weekly positives from me:

- To be sure our team hears and reads something positive every week.
- To be sure our team hears and reads something that builds our culture.
- To reinforce our culture.

There are several levels of structure (supervisors, managers, executives and hourly) in our team that receive the weekly positive. I do this so everyone has a chance to do their part to apply our culture to their job. My desire is that every team member be successful. My hope is the more I define the culture at Master Wall, the better the chance it is applied to people's careers.

I loved what Truett Cathy of Chick-fil-A was quoted as saying, "We are not in the chicken business, we are in the people business." Although we are not in the retail or restaurant business, this still applies to Master Wall.

More Truett Cathy: Truett always believed if you could select the right person again and again, that the collection of the character, competency and chemistry of these people would develop and strengthen the culture over time.

My hope and desire is that Master Wall team members love and respect each other, and that it is noticed by our customers and everyone we deal with.

MARCH 2021

Team,

It has been a while since I read Jon Gordon's book *Soup*. It's a really good book about team and culture.

Here is a quote:

"Lead with Optimism"

"In fact, the research confirms that optimistic salespeople outperform pessimistic salespeople. Optimistic leaders are able to garner the support of others. And positive organizations outperform negative organizations. Same industry. Two companies. The positive one will outperform the negative one."

At Master Wall, we are the positive one.

***

Team,
From the book, *The Culture*

- "... if someone cannot buy into the values of character, excellence, and respect, do you really want them on your team? My experience is that people who practice excellence do not work well with people who practice mediocrity. That is why leaders must be relentless in holding people accountable to the rules of the house. Dumbing down the standard destroys morale and creates a culture of mediocrity."

- Albert Einstein said, "If you can't explain it simply, you don't understand it well enough."
- Vince Lombardi used to say, "We will chase perfection, and will chase it relentlessly knowing all the while we can never attain it. But along the way, we shall catch excellence."

***

Team,

Attached is a recent article on giving from the *Epoch Times*. The article emphasizes the many positives and benefits of giving:

- People who give live longer.
- People who give are happier.
- People who give are healthier.
- People who give make more money.

If you are wondering how this applies to you and your work at Master Wall—think about a company that has all of its team members giving, and what a positive impact our giving will do to make *our* culture better.

ABOUT THE AUTHOR

Steve Smithwick is the president, chief executive officer, and founder of Master Wall, Inc., a leading name in the construction and wall systems industry since 1987. With over three decades of executive leadership, Steve also serves as president of Creative Wall Products, Inc. and previously held the presidency of EIMA (2021–2024). Beyond business, Steve dedicated seventeen years to mentoring youth as head coach of the Calvary Christian School High School Boys Basketball team. His leadership extends to numerous board roles, including Calvary Ministries, the Gardens Assisted Living & Memory Care, and Calvary Christian School. A devoted family man, Steve has been married to Donnie Smithwick since 1973. Together, they have four children, twelve grandchildren, and one great-granddaughter. Steve's enduring commitment to faith, family, and professional excellence continues to inspire those around him.

CONNECT WITH STEVE SMITHWICK

Steve Smithwick lives in Fortson, Georgia, and is pleased to connect with his readers professionally and socially!

Website: https://steve-g-smithwick.com/
LinkedIn: https://www.linkedin.com/in/steve-smithwick-a8aa4b29/
Facebook: https://www.facebook.com/steve.smithwick.16
Instagram: https://www.instagram.com/steve.smithwick.16/#

For professional and media inquiries, speaking engagements, and questions about Steve Smithwick; *Believer, Bulldog, Coach*; or Master Wall, Inc.® you can reach him directly at http://steve-g-smithwick.com.